CHANGED MIND CHANGED HEART

CHANGED MIND CHANGED HEART

A SERVANT-LEADERSHIP COACHING MODEL

MERIUM LEVERETT

TATE PUBLISHING
AND ENTERPRISES, LLC

Changed Mind, Changed Heart
Copyright © 2016 by Merium Leverett. All rights reserved.

No part of this publication may be reproduced, stored in a retrieval system or transmitted in any way by any means, electronic, mechanical, photocopy, recording or otherwise without the prior permission of the author except as provided by USA copyright law.

This book is designed to provide accurate and authoritative information with regard to the subject matter covered. This information is given with the understanding that neither the author nor Tate Publishing, LLC is engaged in rendering legal, professional advice. Since the details of your situation are fact dependent, you should additionally seek the services of a competent professional.

The opinions expressed by the author are not necessarily those of Tate Publishing, LLC.

Published by Tate Publishing & Enterprises, LLC
127 E. Trade Center Terrace | Mustang, Oklahoma 73064 USA
1.888.361.9473 | www.tatepublishing.com

Tate Publishing is committed to excellence in the publishing industry. The company reflects the philosophy established by the founders, based on Psalm 68:11,
"The Lord gave the word and great was the company of those who published it."

Book design copyright © 2016 by Tate Publishing, LLC. All rights reserved.
Cover design by Joana Quilantang
Interior design by Gram Telen

Published in the United States of America

ISBN: 978-1-68207-916-4
1. Education / Leadership
2. Psychology / Interpersonal Relations
15.10.20

Contents

Part I
Changing the Mind-Set of the Individual

1 Foundations of Servant Leadership Coaching 19
    What Is Leadership? 24
        Transformational Leadership 25
        Servant-Leadership 26
    What is Coaching? 27
    What is Culture? 31
    Summary 33

2 Exploring Personalities and Motivation 35
    Understanding Personality 37
    Understanding Motivation 40
    Leadership Style and Motivation 44
        Charismatic Leadership 45
        Transformational Leadership 47

  Servant-Leadership 49
  Transactional Leader....................................... 50
 Effects on Coaching... 52
 Summary.. 52

3 Building the Trusting Relationship.......................... 55
 Relationship 58
 The Importance of Trust..................................... 59
  Trust Is the Foundation 60
  Confidence to Share 61
  Belief in People.. 61
  No Doubts.. 61
  Growth 62
 Leader-Follower Relationships 62
 Building Trusting Coaching Relationships........... 65
 Moving Forward in the Coaching Relationship... 68
 Summary.. 69

4 Developing a Learning Environment 71
 The Learning Environment................................. 73
 What is Organizational Learning?........................ 73
 Learning Affects Change 74
 Creating the Learning Environment.................... 76
 Supportive Learning Environment....................... 77
  Psychological Safety Zone 78
  Appreciate Uniqueness 78
  Open to New Ideas *79*
  Reflection Time... *79*

  Concrete Learning Processes and Practices...... 80
  Leadership Reinforces Learning...................... 82
 Developing the Learning Environment
 and Coaching... 83
 Summary... 84

Part II
Developing the Leaders to Live the Changes

5 Learning to Listen and Communicate Effectively... 91
 Listening Skills 94
  People-Oriented Listeners............................... 95
  Content-Oriented Listeners 96
  Action-Oriented Listeners............................... 96
  Time-Oriented Listeners................................. 97
  Appreciative Listening..................................... 99
  Critical Listening... 99
  Relationship Listening................................... 100
  Discriminative Listening 101
 Communication 107
 Coaching Communication 109
 Summary... 110

6 Developing Ethical Leadership with Core Values...111
 Unethical Behavior... 113
 The Priority of Ethics... 114
 Values Defined 115
 Organizational Values 118

  Developing a Value-Based Culture...................... 119
  Coaching for Value Change 122
  Summary.. 123

7 Clarifying the Vision in Terms
 of Strategic Planning.. 125
  Understanding Vision 127
  Creating Vision 129
   Sole Leader Development............................... 130
   Leadership Team Development 130
   Leader-Follower Shared Development 130
   Collaborative Organizational Development... 131
  Keeping the Vision in Strategic Planning 132
  Visual Thinking.. 132
  Visual Leadership.. 133
  Visual Thinking Leaders Create Vision Strategy 135
  Coaching the Vision.. 136
  Summary.. 137

8 Facilitating Change While Being Accessible 139
  The Importance of Accessibility 141
  Levels of Accessibility According
  to Leadership Style 143
   Transactional Leader....................................... 143
   Transformational Leader 144
   Servant-Leader... 145
  Change, Accessibility, and the Servant-Leader... 146
  Coaching Change Accessibility............................ 151
  Summary.. 152

Part III
Cultivate the Culture to Make Enduring Changes

9 Inspiring Others Through Empowerment 159
    Servant-Leadership Empowers 165
    Coaching Leaders to Empower Followers.......... 167
    Summary... 171

10 Supporting the Community
Through Cultural Awareness 175
    What's the Big Deal About Culture? 177
        Socioethnic Culture 179
        Organizational Culture 180
        Generational Culture 180
    Cultural Intelligence... 181
        Knowledge CQ... 183
        Interpretive CQ.. 184
        Perseverance CQ.. 186
        Behavioral CQ... 187
    Coaching with Cultural Intelligence 188
    Summary... 189

11 Showing Genuine Concern to the Community..... 191
    Emotional Intelligence....................................... 193
    Genuine Concern... 194
        Communication... 195
        Show Kindness 196
        Show Hospitality and Discretion.................. 197
        Learn and Accept Other Cultures 198

Cultural Diversity	199
Awareness of Individual Cultures	200
Cultural Factors	201
Concern for Coaching	206
Summary	207
12 Encouraging Change	**209**
What to Do Next	211
The Resistance Movement	212
Keeping on Getting the Same Old Things	213
Planning for a Change	215
Steps to Change	216
Serving Through Encouraging	218
Identify Positive Potential in People and Situations	219
Communicate Recognition, Progress, and Contributions	219
Communicate With Collaboration and Cooperation	220
Committed to Coaching and Feedback	220
Summary	220
13 Servant-Leadership Coaching	**223**

Preface

We live in a world of hustle and bustle, everyone trying to get to one place or another and doing everything in a hurry. In the process, we tend to treat people differently. We rush and push them and come across as only concerned about our needs. In looking back over history, there have always been individuals who were only concerned about their needs, but the world appeared to move at a slower pace. People did not appear to be in such a hurry. What has all this hurried life done for our leadership, our followership, and our general care for one another? Have the advances of this world helped us or turned us into cold nations of people who feel that others get in our way?

This change in how we view and treat others is why I have written this book. It is my sincere prayer that all readers will take to heart each chapter and engage a leadership coach to help them implement servant-leadership not just for themselves but in their organizations, taking our organizations back to where God intended for them to be—organizations that focus on and serve the needs of others first before serving their own needs.

When we look at servant-leadership, we tend to focus on the word *servant*. But if we focus more on leadership with an understanding that as true servant-leaders, we will serve the needs of the people, then we can better understand the term *servant-leadership*. Serving others is not simply waiting on them like waitstaff in a restaurant. Truly serving others is a way of meeting their needs. Sometimes being a servant is simply offering a smile when someone is facing adversity, offering a listening ear, giving a hug, or just being nice to others.

Making a change to be a servant-leader means that you greet your customers or members with a smile. You take a moment to hear what they are saying, not just herd them through the process. You help that older person fill out the paperwork, you explain why he or she has such a long wait in the doctor's office, or you give your full attention. Being a true servant-leader, you give attention to the little details.

This book was written to help leaders understand servant-leadership, how being a servant-leader can increase the organization's effectiveness, and how a leadership coach can help the leader become a servant-leader. This book presents the servant-leadership coaching model that coaches the leader through the process of becoming a servant-leader. There are three stages to the servant-leadership coaching model: (1) change the mind-set, (2) develop the leader, and (3) change the culture of the leader and/or organization.

In "change the mind-set," the leader learns how personalities and motivations play a role in the leader-follower relationship, and how to take that information and build trusting relationships, which is foundational to the coaching partnership. As leaders build a trusting relationship with the coach, they will take what they have learned and utilize it in building a trusting relationship with the client or member of the organization. This information will also be useful in turning the organization into a learning environment where other servant-leaders can be raised up. Changing the mind-set of the individual will bring the individual leader back to a place to understand that people need people, and serving others' needs first is more gratifying than any other reward.

After the leader has worked through the stage of changing the mind-set, the model takes them into the next phase of developing the leader. Developing leaders is more than teaching leaders how to manage people. It is about developing their communications skills, identifying core values, clarifying vision, and learning to be accessible, particularly through change. Too many organizations, especially churches, place people in a role of leadership without equipping them to lead successfully. Through working with a leadership coach, leaders can be developed to better understand how to help people help themselves.

Next we change the culture of the organization through empowering the clients and members, showing genuine concern, supporting the community, and encouraging healthy change. Coaches are change agents. Through leadership coaching, servant-leaders develop an understanding for individual cultures and how these subcultures build into a larger culture—the organization. By changing the culture of the organization to be more mindful and understanding of individuals, we develop servant-leaders among the people who in turn help one another.

This model was birthed out of three years of working in and attending a church, watching people go through the motions of seeking a better life and circumstances, needing a glimmer of hope, and returning the next week in the same shape as the week before. It was birthed out of going into doctors' offices month after month and watching the way patients, including me, were being treated—as though we were a burden, not a person. This model was birthed out of a deep-seated need for change not only in my own life but in the world. The world needs more servant-leaders to teach others how to care for one another and to transform our organizations. I hope that at least one church, one doctor's office, one retail chain, or one person is changed by this book and model and knows he or she can make a difference. He or she can make a change.

Part I

Changing the Mind-Set of the Individual

The world as we have created it is a process of our thinking. It cannot be changed without changing our thinking.

—Albert Einstein

1

Foundations of Servant Leadership Coaching

As we zoom here and run there, chase a job, reach for success over there, and jet to the next opportunity, we tend to forget to take care of our greatest assets in this life—people. We are all guilty at some time or another of stepping on someone or forgetting someone in our struggles to keep up with our day-to-day activities. Taking a break from work one day, I read a story on the Internet that reminded me just how much we forget the other person. I found several versions of the story in my hunt for the author. Some versions spoke of five hundred attendees, some fifty. But the gist of the story was the same:

> Once a group of 500 people were attending a seminar. Suddenly the speaker stopped and decided to do a group activity. He started giving each person a balloon. Each person was then asked to write their name on it using a marker pen. Then all the balloons were

collected and put in another room. The people were then let into that room and asked to find the balloon which had their name written on it within 5 minutes. Everyone was frantically searching for their name, colliding with each other, pushing around others and there was utter chaos. At the end of 5 minutes no one could find their own balloon.

Then, the speaker asked each person to randomly collect a balloon and give it to the person whose name was written on it. Within minutes everyone had their own balloon. The speaker then began, "This is happening in our lives. Everyone is frantically looking for happiness all around, not knowing where it is. Our happiness lies in the happiness of other people. Give them their happiness; you will get your own happiness. And this is the purpose of human life…the pursuit of happiness." (Author unknown)

Over time, while in pursuit of our own happiness, we have forgotten the purpose of human life. That purpose is to please God and help others, whether it be something as simple as smiling, offering great customer service, or walking beside others as they reach for their goals.

World populations are growing, technology is making travel and communication inexpensive and simple, and attitudes about how to do business and values in business are changing daily. Societies across the globe are becoming filled with self-absorbed leaders and followers alike. What is sparking such a change? Why are people moving away from the old adage, "Do unto others as you would want them to do unto you"? What does this mean for our future organizations? And how can we fix the problem?

These questions are being asked by leaders of all types of organizations across the nations. While there may be options for addressing the problems, they all point to one method—change! The answer lies in changing the way we do business, set goals and objectives, and seek success. If we desire to see a return of trust in the leaders of our organizations, then change is inevitable one industry at a time. In implementing change according to the needs of the industry and one at a time, I believe we would see a domino effect eventually affecting organizations all across the globe. As one organization changes in that industry and shows vibrant growth, another would seek what made that organization successful and evoke change, starting a trend to revamp the entire industry.

At this point, you are probably asking how we, the leaders of these industries, can implement such change. It's through a new coaching model called *servant-leadership coaching*, changing the way we develop leadership in service organizations such as our churches, nonprofit organizations, the health care industry, and eventually customer service-based organizations. Utilizing leadership coaching tools, we can create a new perspective in leadership where leaders are responsible for their growth, goal setting, and ultimately improving the organization as a whole. But it is not only about creating a new *me* perspective in the leader; it is about developing leaders who care about those they lead. We need to develop servant-leaders who place more emphasis on the follower than on themselves. I propose this be done through coaching.

Leadership coaching models typically take the shape of how to improve the organization by improving the leader through proven techniques of coaching. However, for those dealing with people and the needs of people, there is one common denominator missing—the service or servant portion of organization. Service organizations were built on building trust with their customers and providing a service to the customer, including churches and nonprofits. Without people, there is no need for these organizations. So why is it they appear to have stopped emphasizing on customer service, meeting needs of individuals, and treating individuals with compassion and kindness?

In August 2014, Bain & Company published an article on their Web site. It stated that in a "study of 362 companies, 80% of management teams felt they delivered a better customer experience than rivals, but only 8% of customers agreed."[1] This statistic identifies a breakdown somewhere between customer and company. It would appear that customer service has become a thing of the past. Even with many of the organizations in which the theory of servant-leadership was birthed, such as churches, we are hearing more about the leader and his or her success than about the actual congregational members. We hear how successful the church is because of how successful the leader has become. How successful would they be without members? No service organization would exist without the customer.

The servant-leadership coaching model being introduced here works to change the culture of the organization by changing an individual's mind-set and developing the leadership to be more servant-oriented. Although this model is adaptable in secular organizations, through biblical principles of ethics and values, emphasis would be removed from the leader and put on the customer as originally intended. Leaders would become better leaders, receiving self-gratification from empowering others and serving followers or customers rather than promoting themselves or the organization. A natural progression of promotion would then take place.

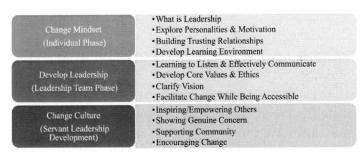

Figure 1. The servant-leadership coaching model.

The servant-leadership coaching model is made up of three important stages: changing the mind-set of the individual, developing the servant-leader, and changing the culture of the organization. Culture is the key to servant-leadership coaching. Moving from a *me mentality culture* to a *servant mentality culture,* we must

- Change the mind-set.
- Develop the leadership.
- *We* then change the culture to one of a servant-leadership culture!

To understand the servant-leadership coaching model, we must explore leadership, types of leadership, definition and history of coaching, and definition of culture.

What Is Leadership?

The study of leadership dates back to the mid-1800s, when Frederick Taylor was a central figure in the development of leadership thought. Taylor began his studies during the Industrial Age of America, a time when industry in the United States was ready for better ways to produce and market products as technology was advancing, markets were growing, labor groups were restless, and there was a lack of knowledge in the area of management.[2] The development of leadership theories progressed through today with the leading pioneers of the early twentieth century making some remarkable strides in building leadership into what it is today.

Leadership is critical in ensuring an organization's sustainability. A fundamental requirement for success in any organization is continuity, though true leadership has nothing to do with the position one holds in an organization. There are many people in the world who hold high-ranking positions but are not true leaders. Leadership is about selecting, influencing, equipping, and empowering followers to meet the goals and objectives of the organization.[3]

The strength of leaders is dependent on how they gain support from the follower and the type of leadership characteristics and skills they display. Researchers have studied leadership styles for decades and have developed numerous styles of leadership that are in place in various types of organizations. The two styles of leadership that are important in implementing the servant-leadership coaching model are transformational leadership and servant-leadership.

Transformational Leadership

Transformational leadership is the ability to motivate, encourage, and stimulate through inspiration. This style of leadership practice influences followers to achieve goals and increase confidence, commitment, and job performance. A relationship or sense of identification with the leader develops among followers that results in acceptance of the leader's vision and values, and goal achievement becomes the norm.

Transformational leaders are most likely to focus on the organization's goals and use charismatic methods of influence such as vision and inspiration to transform followers.[4] While the outcomes of transformational leadership might suggest focus is on the individual, the overall influence demonstrates change in the follower with the main focus remaining on the organizational goals and objectives. What is best for the organization is at the forefront of change.

Servant-Leadership

Servant-leadership, a concept developed by Robert Greenleaf, is about the follower. Servant-leadership can be defined "as a leader's desire to motivate and guide followers, offer hope, and provide a more caring experience through established quality relationships."[5] Servant-leadership places emphasis on the well-being of the follower before that of the leader. The leader behaves ethically, encouraging and empowering followers to grow and succeed not only personally but professionally. These definitions place servant-leadership as the preferred method of leadership for nonprofit or volunteer organizations.

However, there is room for servant-leadership in all sectors of industry, as the biblical examples of leadership call for serving the follower, meeting the needs of the follower, and putting those needs above those of the leader as long as the organizational goals are being met. Servant-leadership, empowering the growth of the follower, fits well within the constructs of coaching.

What is Coaching?

Coaching is rising in popularity as the go-to strategy for leadership development and change in complex environments.[6] According to Tony Stoltfuz, "Coaches are change experts who help leaders take responsibility for their lives and act to maximize their own potential."[7] In defining the coach, he or she is someone who uses coaching knowledge, skills, and abilities without the responsibility, accountability, or authority of the outcomes of the person being coached.

This is accomplished while seeking to cogenerate well-being, purpose, competence, and awareness as a result of a coaching interaction.[8] The coach helps clients search deep within themselves to determine their dreams and set goals. For leaders, goals can be either individual and/or organizational. As the coach and leader proceed through the process, the coach becomes an accountability partner with the leader. However, it is important to understand that at no time does the coach offer advice, attempt to fix problems, or determine goals for the client. Believing in individuals and their abilities helps in developing and empowering leaders to help themselves.

While the term *coaching* holds different meanings for different people based on perspective, intended recipients, objectives, and setting, coaching can be defined as unlocking individuals' potential to maximize their performance, turn their dreams into reality, and help them reach goals in a timely manner.[9] Other definitions include (a) a short-term relationship for providing feedback on areas requiring change, (b) a one-on-one relationship of trust aimed at fostering learning and professional growth, where such relationships provide the impetus for professional breakthroughs, (c) significant change in practice achieved through increased personal growth, and (d) one-on-one relationships for the purpose of enhancing one's behavioral change through self-awareness and learning how to create success for the individual and the organization.[10] The basic premise is the same for everyone, a type of personal training in which the product is empowering the leader within while believing in the person.

The term *coaching* is derived from a French term for moving a valued person from one point to another.[11] The French term refers to travel such as by stagecoach, yet the meaning fits well into the current context of moving people from where they are to a future goal, a better place. Researchers have proposed the earliest form of coaching can be traced back to Socrates some 2,400 years ago.[12] Through his use of dialogue and questioning, Socrates was able to elicit greater insight and understanding through reflective reasoning and questioning. This process is still used today to enhance self-confidence in one's ability to reason by encouraging ordinary human reflection in a coaching setting.[13]

Through the twentieth century, coaching developed into the professions it is today with different meanings for different outcomes. In the same way athletic and performer coaches direct team strategy, life and leadership coaches facilitate individual and organizational strategy. Life and leadership coaching experienced another major boost in popularity with the development of Whitmore's GROW model as published in his book, *Coaching for Performance*. GROW—*g*oal, *r*eality, *o*ptions, and *w*ill—was the most influential and adaptable model of coaching.[14]

Professional coaching is seen as a tool to assist the individual, in this case the leader, in meeting personal and professional goals, retain leadership talent, support succession planning, and improve individual and organizational performance.[15] Contemporary organizations, including nonprofit organizations, are recognizing the need to develop leader competencies that enhance leaders' capacity to understand and distinguish their feelings, manage their behavior, and manage relationships.[16]

With us living and operating in a world evolving at an unprecedented rate with new trends and new strategies developing every day, there is a need to understand human behavior and change the way we conduct ourselves with others. The degree to which leaders will be able to meet these new trends and strategies will depend on their abilities to forgo the status quo and lead with courage, taking risks and embracing change.[17] Skills and attitudes in leadership development are shifting from that of maintaining the status quo, to leading with commitment to the organization's mission and constantly growing to meet the challenges of changing organizational needs while leading with a heart for the people.[18]

Training alone is not enough when developing leaders to meet these new challenges. Coaching can aid in cultivating new attitudes and behaviors to move leaders from the ways of thinking and acting that were common, workable, and dependable in the past, creating a shift to generate new perspectives, different outcomes, and a changed future. Coaching is increasingly seen as a part of the solution for sustainable change.[19]

When used as a long-term strategy to execute an organization's mission, coaching has been widely believed to influence positive leadership, increase charismatic behaviors, and inspire and affect followers.[20] Coaching support provides leaders and potential leaders with a safe environment to learn how to creatively manage change and conflict, improve communication, strengthen self-confidence, retool skills, and foster multicultural relationships in a positive, constructive way by emphasizing action, accountability, and personal responsibility,[21] ultimately changing the culture of the organization.

What is Culture?

Culture is an elusive conceptual design that shapes everything we do.[22] We can define culture in the same way we define air. We know what it is, we live in it, and it lives in us; we cannot see it, yet we know it is there. While there are numerous technical definitions of culture, they do not necessarily give us greater understanding of what it is and how it daily affects us.[23] Culture is something we live in every day. It is considered the anthropologist's label for the sum of distinctive characteristics of a community, region, or nation's way of life. Furthermore, it is more than language, dress, and food customs. Culture "is the conceptual design, the definitions by which people order their lives, interpret their experiences, and evaluate the behavior of others."[24] Other definitions of culture include the following:

> The artificial, secondary environment superimposed on the natural.[25]
>
> A pattern of thinking, feeling, and reacting to various situations and actions.[26]
>
> The shared understandings people use within a society to align their actions. Becker tells us it is defined, created, and transmitted through interaction, it is not interaction itself, but the content, meanings, and topics of interaction.[27]

> It is the collective programming of the mind that distinguishes the members of one group from another. It is the software behind how we operate.[28]
>
> It is the way a group of people solve problems and reconcile dilemmas.[29]

Metaphorically speaking, culture is an iceberg. One can see the artifacts in culture such as foods, eating habits, gestures, music, economic practices, dress, use of physical space, worship, art, and more. However, these areas are only on the surface areas of what we see. Getting people to look below the surface to see the most significant aspects of cultures is the challenge.

Cultural groups share race, ethnicity, and nationality. But people fail to comprehend that a cultural group also arises from segments of generation, socioeconomic class, sexual orientation, ability and disability, political and religious affiliation, language, and gender. Even though human behavior occurs within particular cultures, within socially defined contexts, cultures are always changing. Furthermore, they relate to the symbolic dimension of life or the place where we are constantly making meaning and enacting our identities.

Culture is learned and shared one with another in a process where people perceive and respond to one another in culturally conditioned ways. Cross-cultural anthropologist Edward Hall stated,

> Most of culture lies hidden and is outside voluntary control, making up the warp and weft of human existence. It penetrates to the roots of an individual's nervous system and determines how he perceives the world. Even when small fragments of culture are elevated to awareness, they are difficult to change.[30]

Summary

In summary, in order to effectuate sustainable growth and success, there is a need for change in the way our organizations are led and in the culture in which they exist. A changed mind-set will ultimately lead to a change in behavior and practices in leadership development. By developing a new mind-set in leaders who understand the need to be not just leaders but servant-leaders, we can create a better organization that meets the needs of the customer or member. That organization will surpass all expectations, goals, and objectives. These changes can be implemented through servant-leadership coaching, where the main focus is on changing individual mind-sets, developing leaders, and ultimately changing the culture of the organization.

By using coaching tools and practices, leaders can learn to lead the workforce instead of just managing the workforce, both employed and volunteer. They will reconnect with the people, learn who they are and what they are about, and show them they understand their needs. Leaders and followers will reconnect, which will grow the organization and make it more sustainable in future changes. Coaching to develop a servant mind-set in leaders will change the culture of the organization. Kindness is contagious. Once other organizations see the success of those organizations utilizing the principles of the servant-leadership coaching model, they too will seek change. Change the mind-set, develop the leader, and experience the culture change.

2

Exploring Personalities and Motivation

I am not afraid...I was born to do this.

—Joan of Arc

Motive and personality: the driving forces for what humans do, why we do it, and how we accomplish it! One of my favorite pastimes is to sit in a mall or airport and watch the people. It is fascinating to observe the different personalities interacting in public places, parents tending to children, happy customers, angry customers, and people simply on a mission with no time for idle chatter.

Another place where I love to study personality traits is within my own family. All three of my children have such different personalities. Two are quite reserved young adults who go to work, come home, and answer the basic "it was good" to my "how was your day?". They never elaborate on who they saw or what was said unless asked a direct question. They love the outdoors, are constantly reading when not working, and pretty much keep to themselves with one or two close friends. And then there is the baby of the family, my little social butterfly. She meets no stranger and loves people of all ethnicities, hates the outdoors, does not like to get dirty, and takes an hour each day to tell me all about her day and who said what and went where. She has literally hundreds of friends all over the world and loves to travel. So how did one set of parents have three children with such vastly different personalities?

Change Mindset (Individual Phase)	• What is Leadership • Explore Personalities & Motivation

Figure 2. Servant-Leadership Coaching Model, Stage 1, Phase 2

This chapter on understanding personalities and the role personality plays in our motivation is the next step in the "changing the mind-set" stage of the servant-leadership coaching model. Our personality determines how our minds work, which more often than not plays a role in our motives. But what really drives us? As clients explore and answer that question, the coach can build a stronger relationship with them and help them become a stronger servant-leader, meeting the needs of their followers.

Studying the personality of others can give us a better understanding of their motive. Once we can, clients understand their personality and motives. We can better serve them as coaches because we will be more equipped to encourage them to reach their goals. In reaching goals, understanding followers, and putting follower needs first, leaders will be in a position to reach their potential.

Understanding Personality

Personality and motivation influence how people think, attend, learn, feel, and act in a social context.[1] The term *personality* refers to individual differences in characteristic patterns of thinking, feeling, and behaving. It is a "dynamic and constructed set of dispositions that causes characteristic patterns of interaction with a person's environment and further distinguishes an individual from others."[2] The goal of the coach in understanding personality type is to understand and appreciate differences between people, enabling them to build a more trusting relationship encompassing those differences. The study of personality focuses on two broad areas: (a) understanding individual differences, in particular personality characteristics, such as sociability or irritability and (b) understanding how the various parts of a person come together as a whole.

Numerous personality measures are available for use. The most widely used is the Myers-Briggs Type Indicator (MBTI).[3] This indicator, birthed from the theory of psychological types studied by C. G. Jung, calculates a person's preferred method of handling life, including making decisions, based on psychological types.[4] Jung believed that studying the basic differences in the ways individuals prefer to use their perception and judgment would offer order and consistency to the random variations of personality traits. The MBTI is also used in organizations around the world to help with career choices, professional development, and understanding and adapting to differences in management style.[5]

Our perception involves all the ways in which we become aware of things, people, happenings, or ideas; while judgment involves our coming to conclusions about what has been perceived. Myers and Briggs determined that if people differ systematically in what they perceive and in how they reach a conclusion, it is reasonable for them to differ correspondingly in their interests, reactions, values, motivations, and skills. Using four dichotomies implicit in Jung's theory, Myers and Briggs identified sixteen distinctive personality types that result from the preferences, as seen in figure 3.[6] As leaders and coaches, if we understand these basic personality types, we can better meet the needs of our clients.

ISTJ	ISTP	ESTP	ESTJ
ISFJ	ISFP	ESFP	ESFJ
INFJ	INFP	ENFP	ENFJ
INTJ	INTP	ENTP	ENTJ

Figure 3. Personality Types (See Appendix A for definitions)

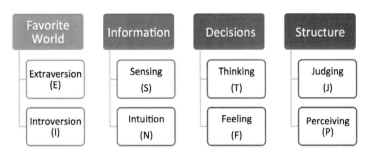

Figure 4. Personality Preferences.

In working through Figure 3, one can determine one's personality type. Favorite world: do you prefer to focus on the outer world, or on your own inner world? This is called extraversion (E) or introversion (I). Information: do you prefer to focus on the basic information you take in, or do you prefer to interpret and add meaning? This is called sensing (S) or intuition (N). Decisions: when making decisions, do you prefer to first look at logic and consistency, or first look at the people and special circumstances? This is called thinking (T) or feeling (F). Structure: in dealing with the outside world, do you prefer to get things decided, or do you prefer to stay open to new information and options? This is called judging (J) or perceiving (P).[7]

When we understand the personality of the one we are working with, we can understand what motivates them. Knowing how they make decisions gives leaders insight as to what motivates them to complete a task. When leaders understand their motivations, the coach can use this information to determine what methods of encouragement and motivation to use in the coaching process. The next step is to understand what motivates people to do what they do.

Understanding Motivation

Motivation is a tricky word. While the word holds the same meaning for everyone, it does not hold the same value for all individuals. What motivates one may or may not motivate another. Everyone is motivated in some way every day, whether it be in getting up and going to work to earn a paycheck; playing a game to win a prize; taking care of family by completing housework, laundry, and cooking dinner to feel good about yourself; or simply reading a book to relax. Everything we do as human beings takes motivation in one form or another, one measure or another. That motivation may be intrinsic—"feel good"—or extrinsic—a reward from outside of ourselves.

This driving force, why we do what we do, is known as motive. Motivation is a process by which our actions are guided and maintained in conjunction with other variables such as "personality, beliefs, attitudes and learning,"[8] Some motivation is good, some bad, but it all comes from the heart. We all have a reason for doing what we do, whether it is to feel good about ourselves or to get a reward.

Determining motivation as a tool of coaching is to understand what guides our actions, how we learn, and what

Changed Mind, Changed Heart

makes us finish our goals. According to Bruce Winston, "Leaders should consciously recognize their motives."[9] They should also understand how their motives affect their leadership style for any given leader-follower interaction. Then they should disclose to the follower what motive lies beneath the behavior in an effort to avoid the follower's misinterpretation of the leader's behavior.

At times, motivation and intelligence are comingled; however, they are two separate processes working together. Intelligence is the purposeful action and rational thinking concerning effective issues of the individual within the environment.[10] Motivation is what defines that purpose, starts us thinking, and causes us to decide whether or not we will work with our environment, ignore it, and do something else.

Motivation varies depending on the situation.[11] While there are situations in which people are self-motivated, there are times when they need to be encouraged by others. When we are self-motivated, we should remember that almost everything we do affects something or someone, especially when performing in our organizations. If we glean an understanding of what we are doing and why, we can ascertain how it affects our followers and organizations in order to determine if changes need to be made.

Leaders can sharpen their leadership skills and build better organizations when they take time to understand what motivates them and their followers. Coaches can sharpen leaders' soft skills and encourage them and followers to change for the better when they understand what motivates them. Mind-sets can be changed to work smarter and more productively to grow the organization.

According to *the evolution of management thought*, individuals are motivated to behave as they do in order to satisfy recurring needs.[12] This "satisfaction of needs" theory is one of the oldest explanations of the reason individuals engage in particular behaviors. "The mere observation of leader behavior may not be sufficient to truly understand the leaders' motive."[13]

Wren and Bedeian continued their discussion of need theory by affirming that the focus of continuing research in leadership has been on the need for power, affiliation, and achievement as motivating factors.[14] Abraham H. Maslow developed one of the most widely recognized need theories of motivation—the hierarchy of needs theory. Maslow determined that individuals are to satisfy five categories of inborn needs: physiological, safety, love, esteem, and self-actualization.

These needs form a hierarchy of ascending importance, from low to high. In his theory, the lower need must be satisfied before the next higher need can motivate behavior. In other words, an individual's need for safety would have to be somewhat satisfied before the need for love could motivate his or her behavior. The strength of a need is determined by its position in the hierarchy as well as the degree to which it and all lower needs have been satisfied.

He also determined that a person can descend to a lower need; however, the process would start all over again, satisfying the lower need before the next higher one could be met. In early studies on motivation and leadership, Maslow was not a lone ranger in his assessment of behavior based on needs and motivation.

James Lincoln, author of *Incentive Management*, appealed to individual employee ambition. He believed that people were giving up their freedoms in order to feel secure, that they were relying on the government to assume responsibility for their security and pride in work, self-reliance, and other time-tested virtues was on the decline. In order to correct this decline, he thought people should return to the *intelligent selfishness* of individual ambition. Lincoln believed that it was recognition of skills that motivated people, not money or security.[15]

There are two types of motivation that leaders and coaches must take into account when developing a plan of action for meeting goals, intrinsic and extrinsic. Intrinsic rewards are rewards or desires within ourselves, not imposed by others, for accomplishing a task for reasons of enjoyment, personal interest, or importance to the individual.[16] Extrinsic rewards are offered from the outside; most are in the form of money or goods. Awareness of these types of motivation and a comprehending of what motivates behavior is key in coaching leaders to become better servant-leaders.

Leadership Style and Motivation

David McClelland developed the motive-based motivation theory that theorized leadership behavior could be understood through three motives: (a) need for achievement, (b) need for power, and (c) need for affiliation.[17] Scott W. Spreier, Mary H. Fontaine, and Ruth L. Malloy of the Hay Group in Boston found there has been a steady increase in the degree to which achievement is a motive for managers and executives, while power as a motivation has dropped; the affiliation motive has remained fairly level.[18]

In contradiction to these approaches, Bruce Winston "argues that motives are 'state' rather than 'trait' and the leaders vary their motives from situation to situation."[19] Winston gave us four leadership styles with four motives. He called these the *me* motive of charismatic leadership, the *we* motive of transformational leadership, the *thee* motive of servant-leadership, and the *it* motive of transactional leadership.[20] Not only should leaders understand these motives and their style of leadership, they should consciously recognize them, understand how they affect leader-follower interaction, and disclose their motives to the follower to avoid misinterpretation of behavior.[21] Let's take a closer look at each of these leadership traits and how they affect the coaching relationship.

Charismatic Leadership

Enthusiasm, charisma, and dedication are some of the characteristics of leadership that create a successful organization.[22] Charismatic leaders are those "who by force of their personal abilities are capable of having a profound and extraordinary effect on followers."[23] They tend to build their own image using self-enhancement strategies. Regardless of whether from western or eastern cultures, the charismatic leader seems to equally have self-esteem and engage in self-enhancement.

Charismatic leaders have a way with words and actions that lead followers to believe they have a right to achieve the vision presented by the leader. Since the goals of the leader are in line with the desires of the followers, the followers seek to expend energy and resources to reach those goals. Winston suggested, "The underlying 'ME' motive of charismatic leadership behavior rests in the desire by the leader to see his/her image enhanced or his/her vision/goals achieved."[24] To remove any suspicion the follower may have about the motives of the leader, Winston suggested leaders self-disclose that they want to enhance their image or they wish to seek to achieve their vision and goal, giving the follower accurate information as to why the leader is persuading them to achieve this goal.[25]

People in many cultures are taught from early childhood to value achievement. Accomplishment for some is an adrenaline rush. When handled properly, it can be an asset to an organization. However, there is a dark side to the achievement motive as well. Over time, performance can be damaged as leaders relentlessly focus on tasks and goals. Leaders who are overachievers tend to command and coerce, rather than to coach and collaborate, which stifles followers.

At times, they forget to communicate crucial information and are oblivious to the concerns of others. Too intense a focus on achievement can demolish trust and undermine morale, reducing productivity and eroding confidence in management, both inside and outside the organization. As the team's performance suffers, morale drops. They risk missing the goals that initially triggered the achievement-oriented behavior. Charisma is thought to be the fundamental component in the transformational process and is described as the leader's ability to generate great figurative power.[26]

Transformational Leadership

Transformational leadership involves both the leader and the follower rising to higher levels of motivation and morality, beyond their self-interests for the good of the group, organization, and society.[27] This style of leadership produces greater effects than transactional leadership in that it moves followers to accomplish more than what is usually expected of them,[28] increasing and promoting follower's motivation, understanding, maturity, and sense of self-worth.

Transformational leaders do what they do in an effort to achieve the organization's goals. By overcoming their personal interest and expecting the follower to suppress their personal interest, it is believed the organization's interests are served.[29] However, this causes the leader's motive to not be clear—whether it is personal or organizational in nature—during the leader-follower interaction, and it is unclear whether or not the good of the organization becomes a means of enhancing the leader's image.

When the leader and the follower do not share in the values and vision of the organization, ambiguity arises. This causes an inability to see a difference in motive for behaviors that achieve the organization's goals. Bernard Bass and Bruce Avolio developed the theory that transformational leaders engage in four elements of behavior called the four *I*'s: (a) inspirational motivation, (b) idealized influence, (c) individual consideration, and (d) intellection stimulation.

Transformational leaders also engage in charismatic and transactional behaviors, but the focus of transformational leadership is on the four *I*'s of behavior.[30]

Inspirational Motivation	Idealized Influence	Individual Consideration	Intellection Stimulation
• Communicate high expectations to followers • Inspire through motivation to become committed to and a part of shared vision • Use symbols and emotional appeals to focus group members • Enhances team spirit	• Strong role model leader – one followers identify with and want to emulate. • Provide followers with a vision and sense of mission • Have high standards of moral and ethical conduct. • Can be counted on to do the right thing. • Followers place a great deal of trust in them. • Highly respected.	• Stimulates followers to be creative and innovative. • Stimulates followers to challenge their own beliefs and values as well as those of the leader and organization. • Encourage followers to think things out on their own and engage in careful problem solving.	• Provides a supportive climate in which they listen carefully to the individual needs of the follower. • Act as coaches and advisors. • Assist followers in becoming fully actualized. • Use delegation to help followers grow through personal challenges.

Figure 5. The Four *I*'s of Behavior.

Through these behaviors, transformational leadership works to improve the performance of followers and develop them to their fullest potential. Those who exhibit transformational leadership traits often have a strong set of internal values and ideals. They are effective at motivating followers to act in ways that support the greater good rather than their own self-interests.

Transformational leaders seek to inspire, influence, reward, and stimulate. Charismatic and servant-leaders do the same; however, the difference is in the motive underneath the behavior. The transformational leader motive is one of *we*, which focuses on the efforts of all for the good of the organization, with the leader's persuasive behavior gaining compliance from the follower.[31]

Servant-Leadership

Servant-leaders seek the greater well-being of followers even at the potential expense of the organization. Greenleaf declared that a leader must first be a servant.[32] Some people shy away from servant-leadership due to negative connotations of the term *servant*. For this reason, it is important to understand servant-leadership is not serving the every whim of the follower or the organization; rather, it is putting the interest and needs of the individual and organization before those of the leader.

Peter Northouse stated the servant-leader has a social responsibility to be concerned with the have-nots and to recognize them as equal stakeholders in the life of the organization.[33] The servant-leader uses less institutional power and less control, while shifting authority to those they lead. Winston presumed "that if there is true values alignment or high degree of person-organization fit, then whatever the employee/follower wants to do will be good for the organization."[34]

In the process of leader-follower exchanges, an ever-increasing bond develops between the leader and the follower. The leader and follower seek what each other wants in a way that the follower begins to behave in ways that achieve the leader's goals. The motive of *thee* is evident in that the servant-leader does not set out to persuade the follower to achieve his or her goals. Instead, the follower sets out to discover the leader's goals and altruistically works to achieve them.[35]

Transactional Leader

In forging the transformational and transactional leadership paradigm, James Burns claimed that transactional leadership is characterized by a *swapping*, *trading*, or *bargaining* motive in an exchange process that lacks durable engagement between the leader and the led.[36] The transactional leader does not individualize the needs of subordinates or focus on their personal development. The transactional leadership style is about getting the task done. In other words, the leader with this leadership style has tasks that need to get done just for the sake of getting them done.

Oftentimes, transactional leaders exchange things of value with subordinates to advance their own and their subordinates' agendas.[37] These exchanges are often an intrinsic or extrinsic reward for the behavior of the follower.

Therefore, the pay offered by a transactional leader will most likely be extrinsic in nature.

According to Winston, the motive for transactional leadership "is devoid of relationship and shows a contrast between the use of 'IT' as compared to the other three, 'ME', 'WE' and 'THEE' as a means of showing that sometimes the leader's motive is not about relationship but about task only."[38] The motive of the transactional leader is evident here just as it is among the other leadership styles. It

may present a persuasive message to the follower to achieve some goal and it may be seen as the leader framing the request within the greater good of the organization or the follower, wherein the leader may really be just engaging in a negotiated discussion or a "telling" discussion as a means of accomplishing a task.[39]

Seeking a relational interaction with a transactional leader may lead to the follower misinterpreting the leader's behavior, which can result in the follower ascribing motives to the leader that are not accurate. Winston called this motive the motive of *it* because it clearly removes the relational aspect from the behavior or the motive,[40] showing the follower rewards are given simply for accomplishing the goals.

Effects on Coaching

The role of the coach is to help the client get the desired result. Many tools are used in this process. Without clear understanding of motives, how motives drive leadership and followership, and how the personality plays into the motives, coaches are setting up the client for failure.[41]

In the servant-leadership coaching model, the coach can better effectuate change, from a transactional leadership to a more transformative, servant-leadership style by helping leaders change their mind-set from that of a task-oriented motive to a follower-needs motive. Without prior knowledge of how personality and motives play a role in the leader's behavior, the coach would not have the necessary tools to invoke successful change.

In addition, understanding motives helps the coach and the leader to determine work assignments, increasing productivity. When people with similar motives work together, they tend to understand each other and want to do similar things.[42] In building a healthy partnership in the coach-client relationship, it is important for the coach to gain a healthy knowledge of personality, motive, and the effects of leadership style when utilizing the servant-leadership model of coaching.

Summary

Motive is the driving force for people meeting their goals and completing tasks. Just as every personality is unique, each individual and task is motivated uniquely. Some individuals complete tasks because of how it makes them feel on the inside to accomplish something, while others seek extrinsic reward to motivate them to meet those goals and complete those tasks. These motives are often driven by the personality of the leader or follower. Some personality traits require feeling as though the leader needs them in order to meet the organizational goals, and that need is the driving force behind why they do what they do.

Such is the case with employees who seek only extrinsic reward. They are paid to complete their job within the organization: take away the paycheck, and you most likely will not see those employees for long. On the other hand, employees seeking intrinsic reward simply complete a task or volunteer to perform a task or reach a goal because it makes them feel good. Different leadership styles employ different needs and motivations. This difference is the process by which leaders motivate followers or how leaders appeal to followers' values and emotions.[43] Whatever the motive, the bottom line is it takes all kinds of personalities with different motives and motivation to get things done in this world.

Now that we have a clearer perception of how our personalities shape our motivations, we can begin to change mind-sets and build the relationships that are so important. Knowledge of personalities and motivations enhances our ability to build better relationships. Servant-leadership coaching is all about developing leaders to be better servant-leaders and coach their followers rather than follow traditional paths of leadership.

3

Building the Trusting Relationship

Trust is the glue of life. It's the most essential ingredient in effective communication. It's the foundational principle that holds all relationships.

—Stephen Covey

The other day, I was watching my son playing with his five-month-old daughter. He flew her through the air and held her upside down as she smiled and squealed with every move he made. Why is she not afraid he will drop her? She trusts him. Then there are the times when my son and his wife leave their daughter with me, and she doesn't worry about whether or not they will return. Again, she trusts them, which is evident when they walk into the room, and her eyes light up and her body trembles with excitement as if to say, "I knew you would be right back."

These events caused me to ponder trust and relationships. This baby has since birth exhibited traits of trust in her parents that are so virtuous. How at the tender age of five months could she possibly understand and trust them as much as she does? Because from birth, she bonded with them. They have not let her down, and her trust in them has grown over the past five months as they have answered her every cry and met every need. This baby has her first relationship built on trust.

It is near impossible to be human without being in some relationship with someone and that relationship not have an effect on us. From the moment we are born into this world, we seek relationship. We are born into relationship when we bond with our parents and then with other adults as they step in to meet our needs. It is true there are those rare occasions when a baby will not bond with a parent, but he or she does bond with someone at that early stage of life. So what happens as we grow and become adults that our trust in others becomes inconsistent or seems to diminish? Why is relationship building a difficult task for some people? What changes that causes people, depending on the situation, to have difficulty developing relationships and trusting one another?

Without visiting the psychological aspects of trust and relationships, it would be a daunting task to begin to speculate on why we as humans interact with each other as we do. The material in the previous chapter of personality and motivation, combined with the knowledge of how trust is formed, will give us a greater understanding of trusting relationships and the correlations of such within the coaching process. It is more important that we understand the importance of building and gaining trust rather than understand why we do not trust.

A trusting relationship is a building block of coaching. Therefore, the lack of such would make the process unsuccessful. It is so fundamentally important that organizations responsible for setting standards and credentialing coaches list relationship building as a core competency of the profession. For example, the International Coach Federation (ICF) listed "co-creating the relationship" as one of the main headings for the core competencies, with the third competency being "establishing trust and intimacy with the client."[1] And the International Association of Coaching (IAC) listed "establishing and maintaining a relationship of trust" as their first mastery of coaching.[2] Both value building the relationship as a building block to coaching.

Change Mindset (Individual Phase)	• What is Leadership • Explore Personalities & Motivation • Building Trusting Relationships

Figure 6. Servant-Leadership Coaching Model, Stage 1, Phase 3.

Building trusting relationships is key in implementing the servant-leadership coaching model. Learning who your followers are and their needs will only come through a strong trusting relationship. Through these relationships, the organization will see growth and sustainability. And through these relationships, the process of coaching will have a positive effect on the leaders, followers, and organization. This chapter focuses on relationship and what it means to the coaching process.

Relationship

What comes to mind when you think of the term *relationship*? When asking that questions many would respond that the term has a romantic meaning. Searching the word *relationship* on the Internet results in Web sites referring to intimacy issues, television advertisements that are about relationships that deal with intimate encounters. But relationship is so much more. It is about human contact and interaction. Some of the interactions are deep; others are shallow. But without them, we are lost and lonely.

Relationships are important in our lives. They connect us to a particular group or event. They exist in all shapes and sizes, from the most intimate to groups with common interest. The dictionary defines relationship as how concepts, objects, or people are connected; a connection or association.[3] Most all dictionaries define relationships in one way or another as mutual dealings, associations, or state of being connected. Essentially, it is a state of connection, being connected one to another for one reason or another. Each relationship we enter into is different or unique, and the trust level in each is different. But they are fundamental to being human.

In their book, *Power Relationships*, Andrew Sobel and Jerold Panas wrote,

> The relationships in one's life are not just important—they are everything. In our business, at home, and among friends, relationships touch our lives in wondrous ways. They are the threads that weave through the fabric of our entire being.[4]

Relationships are a necessary part of who we are and how we function. So if relationships are so important, where does the trust factor come into play?

The Importance of Trust

Trust is key to every healthy relationship. Without it, the relationship cannot grow and thrive. It is like the cement of your foundation. If the foundation starts to crack or crumble, the whole building will become unstable. In the same way, your whole relationship will become unstable. Coaching is no different. Building trust is the key to building the coaching relationship. So why is trust so important?

1. Trust is the foundation on which the relationship is built.
2. Trust gives both parties confidence to share feelings, emotions, dreams, and realities.
3. Trust confirms you believe in the person.

4. Extending trust signifies you have no doubt about the honesty, integrity, and credibility of the other person.
5. Through trust, the relationship is open to growth.

Trust Is the Foundation

Trust is the foundation for all relationships, including leader-follower relationships.[5] When trust is breached, the relationship will begin to break down. When we think about a foundation, we think of something strong enough to support everything on top of it. When the foundation cracks, the integrity of the structure is weakened. Over time, the stress on the cracks causes them to crumble. The foundation breaks, and everything on top tumbles down. The same is true with relationships. When trust is stressed or chipped away, the relationship will eventually falter and crumble.

The breach in trust causes a crack that eventually causes a disconnection in the relationship. It is important to build a relationship on a solid foundation of mutual trust. Clients must trust you as their coach—trust you to keep their information confidential, trust you to guide them on the right path, and trust you to pull them back if they are going in a direction that is harmful to them. Without a trusting relationship, you have nothing to work with, no moving forward, just stagnation.

Confidence to Share

When we trust others, we have confidence in them. We open up and share our feelings, emotions, dreams, and realities. When the coaching relationship is built on trust, we are confident we can share our feelings and emotions. We feel we are in a safe zone. In order to achieve this level of trust, the coach must demonstrate he or she has the competence, system, and processes in place to make one feel safe and trusting.[6] Coaching the transformational servant-leader to become transparent and share stories and experiences with followers will allow followers to relate to the leader and increase their confidence and trust in that leader.

Belief in People

Trust requires we have a certain amount of belief in people. Remember the story I opened this chapter with about my granddaughter? She fully believed her daddy was not going to drop her and was going to return when he walked away. As coaches, leaders, and followers, we must build a relationship built on that type of belief in people if we are to succeed in growing our organizations. Believing in people helps build confidence in them.

No Doubts

Leadership characteristics of credibility, honesty, and integrity build trust in a person. Where there is no doubt of these characteristics, trust is present. Transformational and servant-leaders become role models to followers by gaining the follower's trust and confidence. In listening to the individual needs of followers and exhibiting leadership characteristics such as honesty and integrity, coaches and leaders model examples of behavior that followers then attempt to immolate. Such behaviors nurture an atmosphere of trust.[7]

Growth

Trust and confidence that come from the leader's ability to inspire followers also aids in nurturing the follower's ability to contribute to the organization.[8] Through the steps of trusting and building solid relationships, we see growth within the organization. Success and sustainability become stable aspects of the organization. Sobel and Panas wrote that in order to get trust, we must give trust.[9] Through this process, a relationship is built on mutual trust.

Leader-Follower Relationships

Now that we better understand the role of trust in the relationship, we can focus on some of the relationships necessary to successfully execute the servant-leadership coaching model. This is important to understanding the leader-follower relationship, as research has shown that relationship is linked to follower well-being and performance.[10] A strong leader-follower relationship "endures and involves strong, frequent, and diverse casual interconnections."[11] A good and close leader-follower relationship has high trust, mutual influence, reciprocal liking, and mutual disclosure of privileged information, responsiveness, synchronized plans, and goals.[12]

Leader-follower relationships occur within a specific context. Some of the conditions influencing their behavior may occur primarily or even solely within the work environment. With our world growing increasingly borderless, and diversity in our organizations becoming more the norm, we must take into consideration the cultural aspect of the relationship.

The multicultural work environment requires an understanding of how leadership theory, which deals with human behavior, plays a part in the relationship. In his book, *Leadership: Theory and Practice*, Northouse stated, "Leaders and followers should be understood in relation to each other."[13] Using the global business or organization as a model for how the leader–follower relationship is developed can give us a better understanding of how we can apply the same principles to churches, nonprofits, and service-based organizations.

The cross-cultural transferability in management and leadership theories is subject to the degree of similarities between the cultures. "We should not assume societies which may include indigenous minorities within postcolonial, Western-centric societies or multicultural populations, possess mono-cultural traditions and values."[14] In examining the issues of cultural diversity in the workplace, Kenneth Clark and Miriam Clark found the impact of national and cultural backgrounds on leader and worker expectancies make the tasks of multinational organizations very difficult.[15]

The leader plays a significant role in shaping the culture of the organization. However, we cannot discount the role of the follower in shaping that culture. Even with much disagreement over some elements of definition and measurement, researchers often have agreed that culture may be an important factor in determining how well an individual fits in an organizational context.[16] Putting a leader and follower together with different cultural views, such as being on time, how to conduct a meeting, and people skills requires patience in the learning process from both parties.

Jonathan Goh pointed out leadership theorists "should be more concerned with 'fit' and alignment of their theories to the different contexts and should align their strategies with the organizational design and management systems which are highly congruent and integrated."[17] Person-organization fit proposes an interactional model in which individuals' values and organizational value systems influence each other over time to affect both organizational and individual level outcomes. Without the proper fit in the organization, trust is difficult to build between leaders and followers. Followers must believe in what leaders stand for. Their beliefs and values must be aligned for there to be trust.

Consideration of global concerns, diversity in the workplace, and close leader-follower relationships enhance the successfulness of the relationship. These associated behaviors bring a more harmonious relationship dynamic to the playing field.[18] The use of coaching in building these relationships will aid in changing the mind-set of the individual and open doors of opportunity for cultural change within the organization.

Building Trusting Coaching Relationships

In the same way the leader builds this trust and confidence in the follower, the coach must build a relationship with the leader to gain trust and confidence. The coach understands leaders are the visionaries and set the goals for the organization.[19] A contractual, collaborative alliance between the leader and the coach is created in which the leader defines and sets goals, and the coach helps establish action steps to set the plan in motion to reach the goals. The leader-client agrees to be held accountable by the coach in following the action steps. The ICF expands their core competency to assure the coach understands the importance of the trusting relationship.

B. Co-Creating the Relationship
3. Establishing Trust and Intimacy with the Client—
Ability to create a safe, supportive environment that produces ongoing mutual respect and trust.

1. Shows genuine concern for the client's welfare and future.
2. Continuously demonstrates personal integrity, honesty and sincerity.
3. Establishes clear agreements and keeps promises.
4. Demonstrates respect for client's perceptions, learning style, personal being.
5. Provides ongoing support for and champions new behaviors and actions, including those involving risk taking and fear of failure.
6. Asks permission to coach client in sensitive, new areas."[20]

"To reach their fullest potential, people need both truth and love."[21] Showing people you care is not a difficult task. Being present and paying attention, empowering them to be all that they can be, and believing in people is the first step to helping them reach their full potential. To break it down, there are ten key steps to building a trusting coaching relationship.

Changed Mind, Changed Heart

1. Say what you are going to do, and then do what you say!
2. Communicate. Frequent, honest communication builds trust. Poor communication is one of the key reasons relationships fall apart.
3. Make the right decision. Trust is built one day, one interaction at a time. Yet it can be lost in a moment because of one poor decision.
4. Value long-term relationships more than short-term success.
5. Focus more on your core principles and customer loyalty than on short-term commissions and profits.
6. Be committed. Trust generates commitment, commitment fosters teamwork, and teamwork delivers results. When people trust their team members, they not only work harder, but they work harder for the good of the team.
7. Be honest. Integrity is an important character trait. I often tell my children, "We can work through anything no matter how bad, but if you lie to me we have a new issue because trust will be lost."
8. Let people know you care. When clients know their thoughts, and feelings are heard and accepted in an empathic way, they learn to hear and accept themselves.[22] This will build necessary trust. If they

believe you are out for yourself, their internal alarm sounds, and they will say to themselves, "Watch out for that person."

9. Always do the right thing. We trust those who live, walk, and work with integrity.
10. Be transparent, authentic, and willing to share your mistakes and faults. When you are vulnerable and have nothing to hide, you radiate trust.

Moving Forward in the Coaching Relationship

The coaching relationship as well as the leader–follower relationship are important concepts in the servant-leadership coaching model, as coaching is a form of servant-leadership that involves encouraging or challenging people to pursue their goals and fulfill their potential.[23] The coaching relationship is one that is different from all others. Just as in all relationships, trust is of the utmost importance in the coaching relationship.

As a coach, we should be asking the same types of questions as we become relational with our client. We need to know what our client expects of us and ask, "Who do you think I am?" "What do you seek from me?" These are simple ways to set boundaries and determine what the client seeks from the coach. After the relationship is established, boundaries are set, and everyone agrees on what the job of the coach and the job of the client are. The coaching process can begin. "Don't be put off by an awkward start, find something personal that connects you and you may develop a wonderful relationship."[24]

Within the servant-leadership coaching model, building the trusting relationship is foundational. Without a foundation in place, the model will be unstable and unable to withstand the test of time. By taking the time to build trust and understand trust and relationships from a human behavioral standpoint, the coach can better help the organization meet the needs of the people and, ultimately, meet the goals of the organization. Individual development is a key element in this model, as we learn to put others first and show them compassion.

Summary

We can all say we believe in someone, but until we search deep inside and determine who that person is to us, do we really believe in him or her? Having a holistic view of followers allows leaders to better develop relationships, which gives them greater ability to influence them for the future. By utilizing the servant-leadership coaching model and making the relationship a foundational step, you can change the mind-set of people from a *me* mentality to a *we* mentality and accomplish more.

This model of coaching will put the word *service* back in the customer service. Everything is built on a foundation.

What kind of foundation is your relationship built on? Who is most important in your organization? Are you ready to change the individual mind-set and put the needs of people ahead of the need for material objects?

Keeping the needs of the members of the organization in the forefront and developing strong bonds of friendship, trust, loyalty, and mutual interest, an organization will begin to take on a new culture, becoming unique in a world of self. This is the first step of servant-leadership coaching. A help to building this trusting relationship is to understand personalities and what motivates people. We can then begin to coach people by changing the individual mind-set.

4

Developing a Learning Environment

Tell me and I forget. Teach me and I remember. Involve me and I learn.

—Benjamin Franklin

Why is it when faced with change or growth we tend to reinvent the wheel? We undertake a project or activity without tapping into the knowledge that already exists within a culture or community. While we are blessed with a brain that remembers what we have already learned, organizations are not. That is why it is important leaders spend time and money on learning.

Leaders of service organizations are faced with many challenges in the areas of diversity, constantly developing technologies, migration of nations, and world events. Learning to lead in a servant capacity and teaching others to have the mind-set of a servant-leader is a difficult task in today's world. As leaders and coaches, it is more important than ever to foster a learning environment in the organizations in which we seek change.

When we foster or develop that learning environment, we are helping individuals to grow. Without growth, stagnation sets in. Eventually, we experience a death in an area of our lives. Individuals need nurturing. Learning is available to them to experience growth. Developing a learning environment is the fourth stage of changing the mind-set in the servant-leadership coaching model.

Change Mindset (Individual Phase)	• What is Leadership • Explore Personalities & Motivation • Building Trusting Relationships • Develop Learning Environment

Figure 7. Servant-Leadership Coaching Model, Stage 1, Phase 4.

Learning is the product of structures, systems, processes, and cultures that are indisputably designed to promote learning, which is an inescapable consequence of working and living within an organization.[1] Some leaders tend to think that getting people within their organizations to learn is a matter of successfully conveying a clear vision, giving employees or volunteers the right incentives, and providing adequate training. This assumption leads to taking risk in the face of intensifying competition, advances in technology, and shifts in customer preferences. Key factors in confronting these mounting forces are organizational learning, as well as individual learning.

The Learning Environment

A learning culture fosters an environment of gaining knowledge and improving the organization, as well as the members of the organization, employees, volunteers, and customers. People must take control of their learning in this world of being simultaneously connected at home and abroad. But organizations must move away from training and into the realm of learning. It needs to become an integral part of how the organization does business. Servant-leadership coaching can help the leader develop and achieve the necessary goal of developing a learning environment that meets the needs of the organization and followers.

The concept of developing a learning environment within the organization is not new. During the 1990s, Peter M. Senge encouraged the concept of organizational learning, which resulted in a compelling vision of organizations made up of employees and volunteers skilled at creating, acquiring, and transferring knowledge. These people could help grow their organizations by helping them cultivate tolerance, foster open discussion, and think holistically and systemically, thereby being able to adapt to the unpredictable and being quicker than their competitors.[2]

What is Organizational Learning?

Developing organizational learning and integrating knowledge into everyday practice can be a powerful tool for multiplying an organization's impact, especially as it grows. Organizational learning is a multifaceted concept, which is reflected in the variety of perspectives used theoretically and across empirical research conducted.

This type of learning has been defined as "the development or dissemination of work-based knowledge that is perceived to be useful for improving organizational performance."[3] Many organizations mirror other organization of their type; however, this is not learning new behaviors or practices but rather utilizing old habits of a new organization. Organizational learning is accomplished by sharing knowledge that already exists in the organization and generating knowledge that is new to the organization.

Learning from success and failure is the most common form of organizational learning. Success experience is highly salient and draws attention within the organization, inspiring confidence in ongoing learning activities. This type of learning is subject to behavioral and cognitive prejudices and errors, which are especially problematic when the organization has limited prior success experience. Therefore, it is thought this type of learning may not lead to useful knowledge until sufficient levels of success experience have been reached.[4]

Learning Affects Change

Change is a central element of organizational learning. Some organizations are not thought to learn unless some tangible change in structure, systems, goals, or behavior can be observed.[5] Implementation of strategic change is likely to generate many forms of knowledge, especially when the issue is how to solve problems occurring during the implementation of change and relating to the specific content field of the change itself.

The organization changes when routines are abandoned and new standards are introduced. Two aspects of organizational learning become important when building on basic learning mechanisms: the object of learning and the mode of learning. In regards to learning objectives, the theory of organizational learning focuses on achieving organizational goals through addressing questions of efficiency and efficacy.[6]

Organizational learning utilizes single-loop or first-order learning and double-loop or second-order learning. Single-loop learning describes the establishing of routines by which an organization deals with repetitive tasks. Double-loop learning involves questioning and eventually adapting the objectives of organizational routines. Learning to adapt performance to changing conditions is defined as double-loop learning.[7]

In today's environment, organizations not only have to learn to become more efficient in achieving their goals, they also have to learn how to deal with critical voices from society. When learning includes reflection or sense making, the organization is challenged to change core value assumptions and its specific worldview. Moral organizational learning refers to a change in the dominant values of the organization in making or defending decisions. This transformational learning model has been characterized as *deutero learning*[8] or *experiential learning*.[9] However, not all learning that takes place in an organization is inevitably translated into organizational change.

Observing change may be problematic because there is a lag between change in behavior and change in organizational cognition. Valuable knowledge can result from organizational learning processes without immediately its imposing on behavior in the organization.[10] For instance, the learning cycle can be broken when all the information an organization has is not used for decisions because access to decision processes is restricted, and selling capabilities may be a greater determinant in decisions than knowledge acquired through learning.[11]

Creating the Learning Environment

Creating a learning environment can be overwhelming when leaders feel there is no need for such in the structure of the existing organization. As Senge revealed, developing organizational learning is necessary for organization sustainability. Service organizations do not have to be multimillion-dollar organizations, have multisites, or even have a dedicated knowledge management department in order to benefit from fostering a learning environment.

Through such actions as training staff, circulating meeting minutes, sharing programmatic best practices, measuring the impact of programs, and discussing metrics with the board in an effort to make informed decisions, a learning environment can be created. However, leaders must champion organizational learning; foster a culture of continuous improvement that values organizational learning; define a learning structure that specifies the people who are accountable for capturing, distilling, applying, and sharing knowledge; and design intuitive knowledge processes that are aligned to how people work. This can all be achieved by creating a learning environment that is built through a supportive learning environment, concrete learning processes and practices, and leadership behavior that provides reinforcement.

Supportive Learning Environment

Learning is better facilitated in a supportive atmosphere. Successful learners minimize the negative, reach common understanding with their critics, and adapt to communication and corporate conduct quickly. There are four distinct characteristics to a supportive learning environment that overlap each other: psychological safety zone, appreciate uniqueness, open to new ideas, and reflection time.

Psychological Safety Zone

The psychological safety zone is the place where people can go and feel safe and secure in who they are and what they think and feel. In this zone, they can express themselves without fear of ridicule. Learning takes place best where individuals engage without fear of being belittled or marginalized when they disagree with peers or authority figures, ask naïve questions, own up to mistakes, or present a minority viewpoint. The psychological safety zone is the area where they are comfortable expressing their thoughts about the work at hand and issues that are raised. The culture of the psychological safety zone actually reinforces learning by providing incentives for learning behaviors and by measuring and communicating results of learning.

Appreciate Uniqueness

While all humans were created equally, we were created uniquely, each with our own set of ideas, beliefs, and views about issues. When we become aware of this uniqueness, the learning process begins. We learn about other people, recognizing the value of competing outlooks and alternative worldviews. This new recognition increases energy and motivation, sparks fresh thinking, and prevents lethargy and drifting from discussions at hand.

Open to New Ideas

Taking risk and exploring the unknown are ageless techniques for learning. By opening our minds and being willing to accept innovative ideas, we are opening ourselves to new ideas and creativity. Learning is not simply about correcting mistakes and solving problems but crafting novel approaches. When we as leaders encourage employees and volunteers to take risk and explore the unknown, we are opening a whole new world to them with uncharted waters where dreams can come true and creativity flourishes.

Reflection Time

Reflective learning is the habit of looking back on experiences and reflecting on how you and others thought, felt, and behaved at the time.[12] As technologies grow and we become increasingly dependent on the ability to stay simultaneously connected to one another, we tend to forget to take time to stop and smell the roses.

When people are too busy or overstressed by deadlines and scheduling pressures, their ability to think analytically and creatively is compromised. They become less able to diagnose problems and learn from their experiences. However, when we all take time for a pause in the action and encourage thoughtful review of the organization's processes through supportive learning environments, creative juices flow and learning takes place. It is important to not judge yourself or others for feelings and attitudes, but rather focus on behaviors you will change next time as similar situations happen.

Concrete Learning Processes and Practices

Success and failure can promote useful learning processes. Success can be used to measure effectiveness of current strategies or actions and can facilitate organizations in retaining processes and practices that contribute to success.[13] Business processes of logistics, billing, order fulfillment, and product development work seamlessly to make the business profitable in the same way concrete steps and widely distributed activities cultivate a learning environment in our organizations.

The learning process involves generation, collection, interpretation, and dissemination of information. When thinking about learning in organizations, most people think of problem-solving, education, and training to develop employees. What we don't consider is experimenting with developing new products and services, which includes testing, knowing the product, analyzing competitive trends, satisfying customer, and using current technology. Another consideration for the organization based on servant-leadership is training and educating volunteers and members or customers of the organization.

To maximize the benefit of being a learning organization, the knowledge must be shared in a systematic and clearly defined method. This sharing takes place among individuals, groups, and entire organizations, either laterally or vertically. In addition, the structure should include networks and coordinating tactics that help information flow among the people who need it and when they need it. The central organizing principle is the ongoing reproduction of a commonly shared reality by routines and standards.[14]

The learning process can include importing knowledge from the external environment or from an internal organizational process. While both types of learning are potentially useful for achieving competitive advantage, internal learning processes hold the potential for generating and internally distributing knowledge that is hard to imitate by competitors.[15] The knowledge-sharing process can be internally focused with an eye toward taking corrective action.

In other words, right after a project is completed, the process might call for audits or reviews that are then shared with others engaged in similar tasks. It can also be externally oriented, such as including a regularly scheduled forum with customers or subject-matter experts to gain their perspectives on the company's activities or challenges. This can reduce wasteful organizational search efforts and improve efficiency and performance.

Concrete processes provide opportunities for leaders to behave in ways that foster learning and cultivate that behavior in others. Together, these concrete processes ensure that essential information moves quickly and efficiently into the hands and heads of those who need it.

Leadership Reinforces Learning

Organizational learning is strongly influenced by the behavior of leaders. Theories of adult learning identify behavioral change as a possible outcome of learning. In his model of experiential learning, David Kolb pointed to the four phases of direct experience, reflection, conceptualization, and experimentation within behaviors based on the prior acquisition of knowledge.[16]

Behavioral theories recognize that organizational reactions to success and failure represent an important potential mechanism through which organizational learning occurs.[17] Leaders demonstrating a willingness to entertain alternative points of view encourage employees to feel emboldened to offer new ideas. When leaders actively question and listen to employees, prompting dialogue and debate, people in the institution feel encouraged to learn.

If leaders signal the importance of spending time on problem identification, knowledge transfer, and reflective audits, these activities are likely to flourish. The three building blocks of organizational learning reinforce one another and, to some degree, overlap. Just as leadership behaviors help create and sustain supportive learning environments, such environments make it easier for managers and employees to execute concrete learning processes and practices smoothly and efficiently.

Developing the Learning Environment and Coaching

The servant-leadership coaching model facilitates developing a learning environment by assisting the leader and follower in following their dreams to empower others through learning. Coaching is a learning process. Both the ICF and IAC encompass learning into their core competencies and masteries. The fourth section of core competencies for the ICF is "facilitating learning and results."[18] And the ninth mastery of the IAC is "Helping the client create and use supportive systems and structures."[19] These organizations express the value of coaching, fostering the learning environment and helping clients create that environment within their own organizations.

Whether the goal is expressly to develop a learning environment, the coaching process will foster learning in the leader. Through servant-leadership coaching, the knowledge gained will be shared with followers as the leader becomes more aware of the followers' needs and strives to meet those needs. Servant-leadership coaching will change the mind-set of the leader to understand the value of developing a learning environment that fosters the learning of their followers and reaches organizational goals. The coach employs the knowledge of how individuals learn, combined with aspects of personality, motive, and relationship building to develop a well-rounded program of organizational learning that is fostered by the servant-leader.

Summary

Organizations with the best chance to succeed and thrive in the future are those that see the importance of learning. Whether that learning is single-loop, double-loop, or deuteron learning is not the issue. The issue at hand is that in order to become the best servant-leaders we can become, we must be open-minded to learning and gaining knowledge about the culture, the individuals, and the groups we are called to serve. Then we must share that knowledge with other leaders, teams, and subordinates. In creating a learning environment in our organizations, we create the opportunity to help people grow, understand other cultures, and become a better community and nation.

The servant-leadership coaching model embraces the learning environment and strives to change the mind-set of leaders through knowledge and understanding. It also focuses on helping leaders change their organization to embrace the learning process and encourage other leaders, followers, and customers to embrace learning and become lifelong learners.

Knowledge is the key to human interaction and how we treat one another. Knowledge is the key to changing and growing our organizations. Knowledge is the key to teaching not only our leaders but our followers how to love each other and show the compassion each human so desperately needs in this growing global community we live in.

Part II

Developing the Leaders to Live the Changes

The growth and development of people is the highest calling of leadership.

—Harvey S. Firestone

5

Learning to Listen and Communicate Effectively

The most important thing in communication is hearing what isn't said.

—Peter Drucker

Inevitably, at some point, we all act as though we are listening. We shake our heads, say the appropriate "yes, uh-huh," and even gasp now and then. But do we really listen to what people are saying to us? I thought I was a great multitasker, especially when it came to listening to someone. While listening, I would often read something, type, or keep doing several tasks. What I was actually doing was hearing, not listening. I quickly learned my lesson from no other than my wonderful daughter. It is amazing how much children can teach you.

Being one of those mothers who wants to always be available to my children regardless of what else is going on, I never deny my children the opportunity to talk to me simply because I am working. After all, we mothers know how to listen to our children's daily stories from school or activities, no matter how serious or how trivial, while working. Right? Wrong. My youngest daughter would always start one of her stories with, "Mom, focus!" I would inform her that I could type and listen at the same time. One day, she taught me just how well I do not multitask and definitely do not listen at the level I thought I did.

My daughter has been my social butterfly since she could talk and the one who always had a million things to tell me after school about her day and the people involved. On one particular day when she was fifteen, she started her story. I responded with "Uh-huh. Really? Yes" at different points during her speaking. About halfway through the story, I stopped and asked her, "What did you just say?" She responded, "See! You weren't listening." I replied, "Yes, I was. You just said you got thirteen girls pregnant and that makes absolutely no sense." She explained to me that she had made that statement several words back, in the middle of her story, to prove to me that I was not listening. Had I caught it when she first said it, she would have known I was listening. But because it took a few minutes for my brain to process the statement, that let her know that I had not really been listening to her. I was simply hearing what she had to say.

Out of the mouth of our children come some of the best life lessons we can learn. To this day, we still joke and talk about this story. To this day, she still calls me out on my listening skills and asks if she needs to have gotten more girls pregnant or am I going to focus. While this story could be embarrassing to some parents, I have used it to improve my listening skills.

We all tend to think we can accomplish more than one task at a time. After all, how hard can it be to listen while you work? The truth is that our brains are not equipped to process several ideas at one time. Our brains process items one at a time quickly, but still one at a time. Hearing is a physical ability. Listening is a skill that must be learned and cultivated.[1] Communication is important in all areas of life, but it is a skill to be enhanced in leadership and coaching.

The importance of communicating and listening in coaching is supported by the ICF. Their third competency is "communicating effectively," and their fifth and seventh competences are "active listening" and "direct communication."[2] Due to the importance of communication and listening skills, the first step to developing the leader in servant-leadership coaching is learning to listen and communicate effectively.

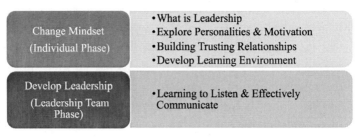

Figure 8. Servant-Leadership Coaching Model, Stage 2, Phase 1.

Listening Skills

Listening is a major component of the communication process. To be a good communicator, one must be a good listener, being active and empathic. In studies on listening, 25–50 percent of what is heard is remembered, while 60–75 percent of oral communication is ignored, misunderstood, or quickly forgotten.[3] It is one of the most important relational activities to maintain and build those relationships.

Genuine, attentive listening has become a rare gift that needs to be cultivated. As we become busier, listening has become a lost art. Listening helps build relationships, solve problems, ensure understanding, resolve conflicts, and improve accuracy. In addition, effective listening means fewer errors and less wasted time.

Changed Mind, Changed Heart

Figure 9. Listening Preferences.

Listening is a process. It is possible to train people to adapt their listening styles to a variety of communication settings.[4] Retraining leaders to listen requires cognitive restructuring, learning new concepts, consistency, and appropriate application of good listening techniques. In the coaching process, the coach helps the leader learn to change his or her learning style when the situation calls for a shift in behavior. There are four listening preferences: (a) people-oriented, (b) content-oriented, (c) action-oriented, and (d) time-oriented.[5]

People-Oriented Listeners

People-oriented listeners exhibit a sincere concern for the feelings of others. They identify with emotional states of human behavior. This preference is influenced by relationship, maintaining a nonjudgmental attitude, clear verbal and nonverbal feedback signals, and allows the listener to recognize the dispositions of others more promptly. People-oriented listeners sometimes avoid recognizing the faults of others, internalizing and adopting the emotional states of others and can seem intrusive and overly expressive when offering feedback.[6] Servant-leaders are people-oriented listeners concerned with what they have to say and the emotion with which it is said.

Content-Oriented Listeners

Content-oriented listeners focus on significant facts and evidence. They welcome complex and challenging information, are inclined to assess everything they hear, favor listening to credible sources, and are able to see all sides of an issue. Content-oriented listeners may discourage other listener types by asking pointed questions and giving too much emphasis on detail. At times, they appear as if they are looking under a microscope and dissecting information.[7]

Action-Oriented Listeners

Action-oriented listeners concentrate on the inconsistencies and errors in messages. They expect others to be ordered and succinct, have a tendency to be impatient and overly critical, get frenzied easily, and at times ask abrupt questions. The action-oriented listener also has a low reserve for energy to listen. This type operates best in an informal rather than formal setting. They give clear feedback concerning expectations and concentrate on understanding the task at hand.[8]

Time-Oriented Listeners

Time-oriented listeners advocate productivity and time management with their self-imposed time confinement sometimes hindering creativity. They tend to become impatient with others, interrupting and rushing those who do not value time, are incredibly direct, let time influence their capacity to focus, let others know how much time they have to listen, and tell others how long they have to meet. The time-oriented listener considers the task to be more important than the relationship with the listener.[9]

Each listening style has its strengths and weaknesses, and it is not unusual for a person to possess two or more strong listener preferences.[10] Listening preferences can change situationally. Listener behaviors are especially influenced by time pressures and relationships. As important as knowing leadership styles, so is knowing listening style. Adapting messages to a listener's cues, it is easier to hold his or her attention, get faster agreement, and build closer relationships.

In addition, this knowledge is another tool for the coach to help the leader make necessary changes to become a better servant-leader. This understanding also allows the leader and coach to train others in how to be a better listener and communicator, skills that people should be enhancing throughout life. Being a better listener helps us be more empathic and understanding of those seeking our help.

Listening can be demanding work. As we listen, our mind has to be active and focused enough to absorb content and implications of what the other person is trying to communicate.[11] This is accomplished by trying to hear what is below the surface, such as the person's feelings, insecurities, self-doubt, conflicts, and discouragements. It is also important to remember that value is not only in what is being said but in what is not being said.

The overall goal is to hear the content of what the person is saying, picking up the attitudes, frustrations, and dreams that are implied. This type of listening has more to do with listening levels than listening preferences. There are four levels of listening that should be developed and nurtured as we grow as human beings: (a) appreciative listening, (b) critical listening, (c) relationship listening, and (d) discriminative listening.

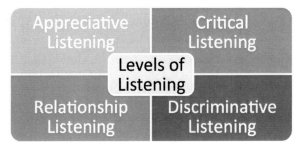

Figure 10. Listening Levels.

Appreciative Listening

This level of listening is simply listening to enjoy the story, music, or information you hear. This level is everyday listening or hearing. This common form of listening is also called informal listening. We practice this level in our everyday conversation. It can be flat and emotionless, enthusiastic, or opinionated and can trigger emotions such as anger and sadness.[12] The listener may or may not pay attention, respond appropriately, or focus on the words and emotions of the speaker. Being the most basic type of listening, it tends to be passive.

Critical Listening

Critical listening is an evaluative, judgmental, or interpretive listening, where the listener evaluates and judges, forming an opinion about what is being said.[13] The critical level of listening involves hearing what someone says, identifying key points and/or arguments, and solidifying your opinion. When you engage in critical listening, your goal is to analyze what the speaker is saying and determine his or her agenda.

This type of listening where "the listener concentrates on what is being said, pays close attention, shows awareness of the speaker and sometimes makes brief comments or asks clarifying questions"[14] is also known as active listening. The speaker knows the message is being heard, and the listener is attentive, which is seen in his or her posture, attitude, and focus. The listener is exhibiting a desire to be in tune with the person speaking. Critical, active, or attentive listening involves more engagement with the communicator and is focused on the speaker.

Relationship Listening

Relationship listening is one of the most important skills to have when dealing with people; it is also known as therapeutic or empathetic listening.[15] As a servant-leader, this type of listening is important. You read the soul and passion of the person speaking. It goes deeper than appreciative or critical listening. This is the type of listening practiced by counselors in seeking to help a client solve a problem or resolve a conflict between two people. It requires honest and open communication between parties.

In addition, relationship listening requires the listener to be attentive, supportive, and empathic. The listener gives the speaker full attention, supports the speaker by being positive, expresses confidence and is willing to give the speaker time, and expresses empathy, not sympathy, to the speaker, which is feeling and thinking with the speaker. Being an empathic listener is crucial to relationships listening.

Discriminative Listening

Discriminative listening is perhaps the most important type of listening for the coach and servant-leader. Discriminative listening, also known as intuitive listening, is when you look past the words you hear to detect the underlying message. The listener has to be sensitive to changes in the speaker's rate, volume, force, pitch, emphasis, and body language to detect the minute nuances of difference in meaning.

Being a discriminative listener combines the empathy and soul-searching of the relationship listener with the identification of key points of the critical listener. To experience empathy, you have to put yourself in the other person's place and allow yourself to feel what it is like to be him or her at the moment. It takes energy and concentration. It is a generous and helpful thing to be empathic, and it facilitates communication like nothing else.

The discriminative listener, being the most important type, combines all types of listening into one and is intuitive about the session, picking up on what is truly being said, not just what is being said.[16] The discriminative/intuitive listener is the person we long for to hear our stories, no matter how trivial they may be. They are the servant-leader, putting their interest behind the speaker and giving the speaker their all. Empathy is the heart and soul of good listening.

Appreciative Listening	Critical Listening	Relationship Listening	Discriminative Listening
Everyday listening	Evaluative, judgmental, or interpretive listening	Also known as therapeutic or empathetic listening	Also known as intuitive listening—look past the words you hear to detect the underlying message
Informal listening to enjoy music, stories, and information	Involves hearing what someone says, identifying key points and/or arguments and solidifying an opinion	You read the soul and passion of the speaker	Listener has to be sensitive to changes in the speaker's rate, volume, force, pitch, emphasis, and body language

Can be flat and emotionless, enthusiastic, or opinionated and trigger emotions such as anger and sadness	Goal is to analyze what speaker is saying and determine his or her agenda	Requires honest and open communication between parties	Combines empathy and soul-searching of the relationship listener
Listener may or may not pay attention	Listener concentrates on what is being said, pays close attention, and shows awareness of the speaker	Listener must be attentive, supportive, and empathic	Combines all types of listening into one and is intuitive about the session
Passive	Involves more engagement with the speaker	Being empathic is a crucial element	Picks up on what is truly being said, not simplistically what is being said

Figure 11. Types of Listening.

Understanding the difference between hearing and listening is a vital skill, whether you deal with people in the boardroom or through comments on your brand's blog. There are ten steps you can take to improve your listening skills and show the speaker you care to hear what he or she has to say.

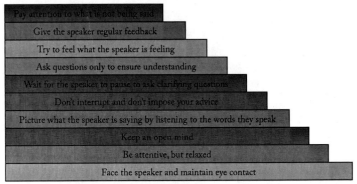

Figure 12. Ten Steps to Improve Listening Skills.

1. **Face the speaker and maintain eye contact.** In most western cultures, eye contact is considered a basic ingredient of effective communication. Eye contact maintains that deep listening skills and removes inhibition of distraction.

2. **Be attentive, but relaxed.** Keep eye contact, but be relaxed. You can look away now and then, but the important thing is to stay attentive. Being attentive means to be present, give attention, apply or direct yourself, pay attention, and remain ready to serve. Screening out mental distractions such as background noises and activities is a must.

3. **Keep an open mind.** Listen without judging or criticizing the things the other person tells you. Indulging in judgmental bemusements compromises your effectiveness as a listener. Also, do not jump

Changed Mind, Changed Heart

to conclusions. Remember that the speaker is using language to represent the thoughts and feelings inside their mind, and you are not aware of those feelings or thoughts until released by the speaker.

4. **Try to picture why the speaker is saying through listening to the words they speak.** Create in your mind a mental model of the information being communicated. Concentrate and remember key words and phrases. Make yourself stay focused on what is being said.

5. **Don't interrupt and don't impose your advice.** Not only is interrupting rude, it sends a variety of messages such as, "I'm more important than what you have to say," "What I have to say is more important," "I don't really care what you think," or "I don't have time for your opinion." When listening to someone talk about a problem, refrain from suggesting solutions. If the speaker wants your advice, they will ask for it.

6. **Wait for the speaker to pause to ask clarifying questions.** Again, do not interrupt the speaker. Allow them to finish before asking clarifying questions. By doing so, you are conveying to the speaker that you value what they have to say.

7. **Ask questions only to ensure** Oftentimes, we tend to get distracted and ask irrelevant questions to the conversation. Be mindful to stay on topic and only

ask questions that give understanding to what the speaker is speaking about.

8. **Try to feel what the speaker is feeling.** This goes back to being empathic to the speaker. If you feel sad when the person with whom you are talking expresses sadness, joyful when she expresses joy, fearful when she describes her fears, and you convey those feelings through your facial expressions and words, then your effectiveness as a listener is assured.

9. **Give the speaker regular feedback.** By reflecting on the speaker's feelings, you show you understand them. If their feelings are hidden or unclear, then occasionally paraphrase the content of the message. The basic premise of this step is to give the speaker some proof you are listening and following their train of thought.

10. **Pay attention to what is not being said, nonverbal cues.** We can glean a great deal of information about each other without saying a word. Even over the telephone, we can tell from a person's tone and cadence how they are feeling or what emotions they are expressing. Face-to-face with a person, you can detect emotions such as enthusiasm, boredom, or irritation quickly in the expression around the eyes, the set of the mouth, and slope of the shoulders.[17]

Improving listening skills can reduce the amount of conflict experienced in relationships, as misunderstandings would be less likely to occur. Listening is a gift to the speaker; it conveys a message of respect, interest, and willingness to connect and understand.[18] As a coach practicing servant-leadership coaching, listening is an important skill to cultivate, allowing clients to know their importance and that someone cares for what they have to say. In developing leaders, they need to be taught to listen to their followers and coleaders, paying attention to details and letting each person know his or her importance in the organization. Listening is the most important tool of communication.

Communication

Regardless of where we live or what we do, there is one element of life that no one can exist without—communication. Communication is a complex yet basic essential element in everyday life. Nothing in life can be achieved without communication, whether verbal or nonverbal. According to William Gudykunst and Young Kim, "We communicate the way we do because we are raised in a particular culture and learn its language, rules, and norms."[19]

Gudykunst and Kim further suggested different cultures have different rules and norms. Understanding the other's culture facilitates cross-cultural communication. As the world is evolving ever so quickly into a diverse multicultural world, it is becoming increasingly essential that we all learn to communicate across the cultures that make up the globe, whether we work and worship domestically or abroad.

Communication is a complex term. As with most leadership terms, it does not have one set or definitive definition. A simple definition would be to transfer information from one place to another. *Merriam-Webster* defines communication as "a process by which information is exchanged between individuals through a common system of symbols, signs or behavior."[20] Although this is a simple definition, when we think about how we may communicate, the subject becomes much more complex.

There are various categories of communication and more than one may occur at any time. Some of the different categories of communication follow: (a) spoken or verbal communication, which includes face-to-face, telephone, radio, television, or other media;

(b) nonverbal communication, which includes body language, gestures, and how we dress or act; (c) written communication, which includes letters, e-mails, books, magazines, Internet, or other media; and (d) visualizations, which includes graphs, charts, maps, logos, PowerPoint, and other visualizations that can communicate a message.

Robert Rosen, Patricia Digh, Marshall Singer, and Carl Phillips gave us two basic goals to communications: (a) to clarify priorities and expectations to tell people what needs to be done and (b) to create the right tone.[21] The desired outcome or goal of any communication process is understanding. Culture determines the communication style of most people. Rosen stated, "Westerners are good verbal communicators; Easterners are good at the nonverbal."[22]

The ability to speak the language of a particular culture without grasping the values behind it could be dangerous. However, having a strong understanding of what drives the culture without the ability to communicate verbally is equally problematic.[23] For this reason, a study of culture is important when developing leaders to become servant-leaders. Understanding others' viewpoints, values, and beliefs gives a clearer path to communicating effectively and avoiding miscommunication. For this reason, communication is an important part of leadership development.

Coaching Communication

Listening is a skill that is imperative to coaching: it is "central to every part of coaching although it is never more important than at the beginning."[24] To the person being coached, listening is a gift, as so many of us in our hurried lives today do not take time to listen to people at the level that makes them feel, respected, interested, and willing to connect and understand.

In addition, when a person feels the other is listening to what he or she has to say and interested in every word, it makes the person feel known and understood. People feel safe and secure when they are listened to, and they begin to trust. The coach listens for positive things such as the client's hopes, strengths, values, passions, competencies, excitements, and dreams that help them build relationships, clarify issues, and facilitate understanding.[25] These are the reasons listening is so important to coaching. Effective coaches are listening coaches.

Summary

Communication is multifaceted, consisting of verbal and nonverbal communication. What people have to say is important to them and oftentimes to the leader as well. When the leader learns to listen to the follower and communicate in a clear and articulate manner conducive to the culture, progress can be made in serving that group of the organization. Listening is one of the most integral parts of communication for not only the coach but the leader and follower. Listening should be important to all people.

Listening intuitively is courteous. It is evidence of care for what someone has to say, giving people the due attention, for their time and effort should be paramount to each of us as human beings. Somewhere along the way, we have lost the art of listening and chosen to put our interest above others. This disrespect of people is causing all sorts of problems across our country. By learning to listen to people again in a caring and compassionate manner, we can return not only our organizations but our country, our world, back to a world that cares for people. People do matter. Listen to let them know.

6

Developing Ethical Leadership with Core Values

It's not hard to make decisions when you know what your values are.

— Roy E. Disney

From the beginning of time, man has struggled with doing the right thing, from Adam accepting the fruit from Eve to the world scandals we see today. For some, honesty, integrity, and treating your fellow human being with kindness and consideration is a way of life, characteristics they live for and strive to live out. For others, these characteristics are not easy, and they must work hard to attain them. Unfortunately, there are leaders today who are not trying to overcome the hurdles, and the values held by our forefathers when they formed this nation, which have been passed down through the ages, are going by the wayside.

Regardless of where a person lives, we see evidence that the values of twenty, thirty, forty years ago are not the values held by people today. With the deterioration in values has been a wave of unethical behavior. Organizations are failing as the leaders fail, and people are losing trust in organizations and leaders all around the world. These are not quiet, hidden behaviors; these behaviors affect people everywhere and must be changed. Unfortunately, the scandals are too many to count.

Ethical behavior and organizational value systems are passed down from leadership. For that reason, we must study how ethics and values are established and set within in our organizations. This is a part of leadership development as many of our values are infused by the leader, and our service-oriented and nonprofit organizations are values-driven. Therefore, the second step to leadership development in the servant-leadership coaching model is developing ethical leadership with core values.

Figure 13. Servant-Leadership Coaching Model, Stage 2, Phase 2.

Unethical Behavior

When discussing unethical behavior and scandals, people are quick to remember the events of the 1990s and early 2000s that involved companies and individuals such as Enron, WorldCom, Tyco, Arthur Anderson, Citigroup, Merrill Lynch, and Bernie Madoff.

The United States is not the only country with organizations and leadership operating unethically. Internationally, there was the London-based pharmaceutical company GlaxoSmithKline that paid kickbacks to physicians writing prescriptions for their products;[1] Johnson & Johnson illegally boosting sales by off-label marketing of drugs for unapproved uses;[2] the News of the World being accused of illicitly hacking into the voice mail messages of prominent people to find stories;[3] and even the Vatican, as written about in the Italian media, was charged with unethical behavior in sensitive documents, alleging corruption and exposing power struggles.

In addition to these examples, there are rampant political sex scandals, lying, and cheating in Washington, and government officials around the world accepting bribes from companies wanting to do business with them. Universities are seeing a rise in cheating, lying, and covering-up scandals involving drugs and sexual assaults.[4] And just as scandalous are the stories we do not see in the media: child abuse, elder neglect, marital infidelity, income tax cheating, mail fraud, and more. Why do we behave unethically? What has changed in the world for people to become so me-oriented and act in such immoral ways?

The world has become consumed with "what's in it for me?" and not "what can I do to make a difference in someone else's life?" Even those who want to make a difference in someone's life only want to do so at the reward of fame for themselves. In consideration of the wave of unethical practices being witnessed throughout the globe today, one cannot afford to be silent about the relevance of ethics and ethical leadership in the twenty-first-century organization.

For this reason, the subject of business ethics has become a leading concern in the minds of the modern-day stakeholder and beneficiary of organizational leadership.[5] Ethics has become considerably essential to organizational leaders. Ultimately, the argument for business ethics is unavoidable and momentous.[6]

The Priority of Ethics

Ethics need to become an organizational priority, more than simply a legal or moral responsibility. To discuss the priority of ethics, we first must define ethics. *Webster's New World College Dictionary* defines ethics as "a system of moral standards or values; a particular moral standard or value." Ethics put forth the following questions: How fair is it? Is it correct? And is it honest or dishonest?[7] It can be viewed as a set of principles comprised of high quality or right deeds that eventually entail accommodating accountability.[8]

But ethics is about values too. Values are defined as "traits, behaviors or qualities to which we ascribe some worth or importance." Joanne Ciulla contended, "Ethics is about the assessment and evaluation of values."[9] She defined values as "the ideas and beliefs that influence and direct our choices and actions."[10] Ethics is about behaving, making choices, and taking actions according to one's values that reflect beliefs about how things should be done. So what are values, and whose values does an organization follow? These are the questions leadership must face every day as people come into the workplace with their own values, which may or may not be similar to those of the person next to them or yours for that matter.

Values Defined

Traditional values are thought to be the foundational ideas about what an individual feels are good or bad, right or wrong, moral or immoral. People who do not think about their values or do not have a strong set of values are more easily swayed by circumstances, fads, and other's opinions. Raymond Boudon stated it as follows, values reflect a person's beliefs about what is good or bad, fair or unfair, legitimate or illegitimate.[11]

Through individuals' values, one can often ascertain how they feel about certain issues or how committed they are to their own personal beliefs. Values are the underlying foundation for ethics, as they help to determine behaviors and set limits regarding what an individual will tolerate or overlook in others' behavior. They root leaders and remind them of their obligations. There is much debate, however, over where values originate and why people hold to the values and beliefs as they do.[12]

Christian leaders are aware their values derive from the Bible, which gives much instruction concerning values and ethics. However, in the past few years, we have been seeing Christian leaders reevaluating and changing their values. In the twentieth and twenty-first centuries, Christian ethic has come under attack. Value systems have their day and then fade away. But those grounded in the Ten Commandments that God gave mankind remain a foundational principle even in the world today.

Whatever people think of these values, they still remain the basis of any system of ethics for the servant-leader, as the sixth through tenth commandments (Exodus 20:13–17) were designed as values system to build a cohesive society. Each of these commandments was based on the value that God placed on people, their lives, their relationships, their property, and their reputation. That helps us to understand Christian values. But not everyone, including all leaders, is Christian. So where do those who do not claim to be Christian derive their values?

We can look to Charles Taylor's position on moral feelings to get a better understanding of values and see from where they are derived. Taylor described values as *moral feelings* that "are distinguished from other feelings by their internal relation to values and to one's self-understanding. Accordingly they would simply not be moral feelings if they were not related to our conception of the good."[13] He further stated our moral feelings relate to our values, and the gap between our moral feelings and reflective values can be bridged through articulation of these moral feelings and reflective values. "When we articulate our moral feelings we give them a form in which they can be discussed."[14] Leaders who identify and uphold their values are more decisive and effective, and their organizations are likely to be more successful.

Organizations do not form spontaneously or accidentally. The beliefs, values, and assumptions of the founder and leaders echo throughout the entire organization, shaping the learning experiences of the members during the start-up phase of the organization.[15] Typically, the organization takes on the personality and shape of the strongest leader. As one leader leaves and another takes his or her place, the organization changes to mimic that of the leader in charge. There are times when such change can be bad. However, most often it is for the better as it grows the organization in a different direction. One can open opportunities to pass these values on, helping others to understand the values we have and why.

The Word of God guides Christians in forming these moral feelings. For example, Colossians 3:5 (New

International Version) states: "Put to death therefore what is earthly in you: sexual immorality, impurity, passion, evil desire, and covetousness, which is idolatry." It is important that Christian leaders understand moral feelings and reflective values and learn to articulate them in order to infuse them into the organizations they lead.

Alain Fayolle, Olivier Basso, and Thomas Legrain suggested, "A value system is an enduring organization of beliefs concerning preferable modes of conduct or end-states among a continuum of relative importance."[16] In other words, a value acts as an ideal principle that people or leaders refer to in order to base their judgment when deciding which course of action to adopt. The beliefs, values, and assumptions of founders or leaders infuse organizations and shape the learning experiences of the group members during the start-up stage. While values typically remain constant, they can be changed, usually for the better.

Organizational Values

All organizations develop a culture based on the beliefs of the leader. The culture developed is simply the "prevailing ideology (beliefs/values) that people carry around in their heads."[17] Many organizations are unaware of their culture as it pertains to ethics and values. If employees were to ask their leadership to define ethical behavior, how many would avoid the question due to not totally understanding their organizational culture themselves? Ethical and value issues stem from the culture in which we live and work. Daryl Green stated, "A large portion of an individual's values are formed in the early stages of life through parents, teachers, family, friends, and his or her environment."[18]

To change the culture of an organization and raise the bar on the standards of ethics, business ethics with mission, vision, values, strategies, and goals must be integrated and aligned. Because of the social nature of ethical values, the alignment process will be concerned with relationships and defining relational expectations between leadership, employees, stakeholders, and customers. The goal of an ethical organizational culture is the greater good of all. Internal relationships between leaders and followers, as well as external relationships with clients, customers, vendors, and the community are all prized. As a result, people are treated well consistently, and an ethical culture emerges.

Developing a Value-Based Culture

Ethics in the twenty-first century are not a luxury, nor are they an option. People at all levels of an organization need ethical value more than competence, experience, intelligence, or drive. Rushworth Kidder expounded, "The principle task of this decade is the creation and nurturing of a values-based culture."[19] People spend a great amount of time at work, therefore, much of the nurturing Kidder talked about must take place in the organization. Kidder identified four key factors in creating a values-based culture:

shared core values, common language, commitment at the top, and moral courage.

Figure 14. Four Keys to Values-based Culture.

- **Shared core values**

    Five core values found in some form in every culture worldwide are honesty, respect, responsibility, fairness, and compassion. A values-based culture will make these core values the driving force in decision-making.

- **Common language**

    Employees need a language of ethics that allows them to communicate readily and comfortably about issues that are typically sensitive and difficult to discuss. Effective ethics training programs provide the common language needed.

- **Commitment at the top**

    Ethics training is meaningless without top-level executives who practice what they teach. When leaders consistently reward those who choose to do what is right, it helps to create an ethical culture more than anything else could.

- **Moral courage**
    Kidder describes moral courage as "the quality of mind and spirit that enables one to face up to ethical dilemmas and moral wrongdoings firmly and confidently, without flinching or retreating."[20]

Servant-leadership coaching aids leaders in weaving together their values and ethics, lifestyle, and culture in a way to not allow them to become separated, showing them a holistic approach to leadership and life, as these three elements constitute how people relate to one another in the home, the workplace, and every part of society. According to Jeff Waller, "A business that does not provide specific ethics guidance to its employees is inviting its personnel to decide what is best for the business based upon each individual's own ethics, rather than the business' core values."[21] In working on ethical issues and what is right and wrong, leaders must consider the globalization of organizations in this day and age.

Due to the rise in globalization, one of the first factors to determine is the culture of the organization and the nationality of the leaders leading that organization. For leaders of global organizations, it is imperative that there is an understanding of the ethical differences between the nations involved. Rafik Beekun, Jim Westerman, and Jamal Barghouti argued that ethical differences between countries has a potential impact of a country's national cultures on ethics and what drives the decision-making process underlying ethical behavior in both countries.[22]

An understanding of these differences is critical toward enhancing ethical behavior in both countries. Edgar Schein pointed out that simply telling a person in another culture that an action is unethical may alienate that person.[23] Understanding the behavioral process underlying ethics across national cultures helps the leader to make sense of an individual's ethical decision-making process and behavior, which allows further insight in avoiding offending others.

Coaching for Value Change

To change the culture of an organization and raise its ethics to a higher standard, there must be an alignment process that integrates business ethics with mission, vision, values, strategies, and goals.[24] The use of coaching to help the leadership of the organization to understand this alignment process and, thereby, line up their ethical practices should be considered when implementing change.

Because of the social nature of ethical values, this alignment process is concerned with relationships and defining relational expectations between leadership, employees, stakeholders, and customers. The goal of an ethical organizational culture is the greater good of all. Internal relationships between leaders and followers, as well as external relationships with clients, customers, vendors and the community, are all prized. As a result, people are treated well consistently, and an ethical culture emerges.

The servant-leadership coaching model utilizes this change to aid in developing the leader. Through helping the leader to understand the importance of values and teaching them to coach the followers, changes to the organization for the betterment of all can be achieved. Values are powerful motivators. The coach helps leaders to evaluate their values and ethical practices and then make sure they align with the organizational goals.

Through servant-leadership coaching, the coach also helps leaders develop values that place the proper attention on people as opposed to placing all their value on financial success and organizational success. I believe that when the value is placed on the human life over that of financial gain and organizational success, followers will be more motivated to move the organization forward, and financial and organizational success will follow.

Summary

In today's highly competitive world, organizational leaders have a lot on their minds. It is important for them to keep abreast of rapid technological advancements, competitors' products and services, the effects of globalization, and opportunities and threats within their own industry, to name the most obvious. In addition, they must keep a constant eye on the mission, vision, values, culture, strategy, and goals of their own organizations. Amidst all of this complexity, finding room on the organizational plate for another major priority is not easy.

However, to succeed in the twenty-first century, organizations have to figure out how to make ethics a priority. Priorities are known as those few things that are deemed most important to a person. While many things are important, some are more and some are less important, with only a few things being most important. Ethical values need to rank as one of the most important success factors in twenty-first-century organizations. As an organizational priority, ethics will affect the organization's culture and decision-making.

It is imperative that leaders today have a firm understanding of their organization's culture, develop a sound value system, and insist on ethical behavior from all employees and volunteers regardless of rank. Servant-leaders meet the needs of people first, making people a priority. Servant-leaders value people more than things. The servant-leadership coaching model, when properly utilized, helps leaders achieve a more successful organization by placing more value on people and less on self-image, financial success, and organizational productivity.

7

Clarifying the Vision in Terms of Strategic Planning

Good business leaders create a vision, articulate the vision, passionately own the vision, and relentlessly drive it to completion.

—Jack Welch

My husband and I have different ideas about our vacations. We agree on the final destination. However, how we arrive at that destination is what we tend to disagree on. I like to drive on back roads, through little towns, taking my time and taking in the sights as we drive along, stopping when I see something that catches my eye and finding new little nooks and crannies throughout the countryside to visit. My husband, a truck driver, likes to plan the trip. He wants to go from point A to point B with the least amount of stops, arriving at the planned time, and not discovering any jewels in the countryside. He is on a mission.

Neither method is wrong, simply different approaches for the same outcome. One may take a little longer to get to point B than the other, but both approaches will lead to the same outcome, which is getting to point B and enjoying our vacation.

In the same way that we must determine the plan of action for our vacations, organizational leaders must plan for the future endeavors of reaching point B and beyond. Do they want to take the road less traveled, taking their time and smelling the roses as they travel the road to success, or do they simply want to get on the interstate and reach the end point in order to have more time to meet future end points quicker? This is a question all leaders must ask themselves.

The difference in organizational planning and family planning is that the future of an organization is determined by the actions and choices made by leadership, with success being a major objective that can dismantle the organization if the objective is not met. If we do not make it to vacation, or have the time we want at the end point of our vacation, nothing detrimental will happen. We will simply be disappointed. However, in the case of organizational strategic planning, not reaching the objective can have detrimental effect on the future of the organization.

Changed Mind, Changed Heart

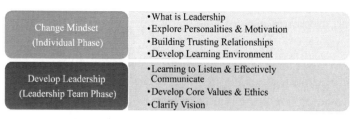

Figure 15. Servant-Leadership Coaching Model, Stage 2, Phase 3.

As we continue to build on the servant-leadership coaching model, in the third section, we explore focuses on clarifying the vision. Without a clear vision, the leader is unsure of where he or she is taking the organization and how to get there. The coach can help that leader to take the proper path, keeping the goal before them, and developing the follower as they go through the journey.

Understanding Vision

Vision is a multipurpose tool for the organization. It gives the leader the ability to see the present as it is and formulate the future[1] that grows out of and improves upon the present.[2] Viewing that vision for what it is and seeing how it catapults our dreams into reality and toward our greater goals gives us the insight to see the vision working as a multitool within our planning sessions. Vision has been cast as the road map to success that leads down the path to success, showing leaders where they are going and how to get there. In reality it is much more, as it guides and motivates not only the leadership but the membership as well.

When leaders have a vision, the farsightedness of the future and the nearsightedness of the present are removed, providing them the ability to remain rooted and grounded in what they believe. The ability to provide vision is a powerful force, as a vision is a target toward which a leader not only aims his or her energy and resources but those of the organization as well.[3] The constant presence of the vision keeps the leader moving forward despite various forces of resistance such as fear of failure; negative responses from constituents, peers, employees, or volunteers; and practical difficulties or problems within the industry.

When shared with employees, volunteers, and other members of the organization, vision keeps the organization moving forward, enabling and inspiring leaders and followers alike. This keeps the organization from experiencing disconnect within the body, as everyone is moving toward the same goal. The stereotypical hierarchy of leadership can be turned into a well-organized and harmonious matrix, working together toward a common goal.[4]

Properly communicated vision creates a force within the leader, which spreads excitement like wildfire. It is an image of the future that can be discussed and perfected by those vested in the organization, a glue that binds the individuals into a group with common goals. Vision defines what you stand for, why you exist, and who your team will become, adding meaning to the organization.[5]

The role of the leader is not only to clarify the vision but to actually create meaning for people by amassing large amounts of information, making sense of it, and integrating it into a meaningful vision of the future. Leaders then communicate that vision in a way that people want to participate in its realization. For the service industry organizations, as well as corporate organizations, this participation empowers the people to take ownership, to feel a part of the organization and not just a by-product.

Creating Vision

Researchers on creating vision have suggested four methods of development: (a) vision created by a sole leader, who also communicates directly to the followers, (b) leadership team creates and communicates the vision to followers, (c) shared creation where visions are cocreated by a leader and followers in a sensemaking and sense-giving process, where the leader proposes the vision that is modified through exchanges between leader and follower, and (d) organizational vision is developed by the organization as a whole engaged in a large group collaborative process.[6]

Vision requires communication; however, the nature of communication differs across the approaches. In the first two approaches, vision is transmitted from upper to lower levels. In the last two approaches, communication during vision creation is central to the creation of shared ownership of the vision by organization members.[7]

Sole Leader Development

Vision is an image created in the mind of the leader in this method of development. Afterward, it is communicated to the followers. In this method, vision formation involves personal experience that entails the ability to isolate key goals or causes that were needed to create a strict mental model. The advantage for the leader in this model is that a suitable vision for the organization can be substantially controlled both within content and communication by the leader. Vision that is developed by one individual must be transmitted to others in the organization through skillful articulation to keep misunderstanding, inaccurate interpretation, and incomplete memory to a minimum.[8]

Leadership Team Development

A study in the United Kingdom showed that two-thirds of organizational visions were developed by small teams.[9] This approach leverages the value of multiple voices and minds, bringing synergy and endorsement of the leadership team to the vision. The two challenges presented in team development are that of most team projects: working together to develop the vision and effectively communicating it to members, followers, and stakeholders.

Leader-Follower Shared Development

The leader-follower shared development method of creating vision is a process in which the leader creates a vision and shares that vision with constituents in order to receive differing perspectives. The followers then interpret and modify the vision and communicate that modification back to the leader. This back-and-forth mutual process continues until a concrete vision upon which all parties agree is developed and then shared with the entire organization.[10]

The challenge to this method is evident in diminished personal control of the leader both in vision development and communication as the vision may not be exactly what the leader initially believed the organization needed. However, the leader is most likely to foster greater agreement, common understanding, and commitment to the vision among followers,[11] which in a servant-leader capacity outweighs the challenges.

Collaborative Organizational Development

Creating a vision as a whole within the organization, also known as collaborative organizational development, has advantages and disadvantages. This method typically is developed by the stakeholders as a collaborative group. It is basically used in private businesses, nonprofit organizations, and public organizations.[12] There are four attributes to large group methods of development: (a) a variety of stakeholders are involved, including organization leaders, workers, customers, and members, (b) multiple perspectives are encouraged through a variety of interactive exercises, (c) all participants are given a voice in the process of shaping the vision, and (d) common ground is emphasized.[13]

Keeping the Vision in Strategic Planning

Creating vision is an important aspect of leadership, and development of a clear vision by leadership is central to strategic leadership and planning.[14] The actions and choices of the leadership, shaped by the clarification of vision, determines whether an organization creates a forward-thinking atmosphere that is prepared for the future or an atmosphere that reacts as change comes along.

Leaders cannot predict the future, so how can an organization prepare for the changes needed to reach future goals and to face uncertainties that lie ahead? The organization depends on strong leadership that does not "focus on managing an internal change process"[15] but instead are visual thinkers who take action in order to ensure success in the future.

Visual Thinking

These explanations point toward looking at the organization in the future. Leaders can shape the future of an organization with their choices and actions by utilizing strategic thinking, insight about the present, and foresight about the future. "The process that stimulates both of these by helping us link our intuitive sense of events in the world with our intellectual understanding"[16] is visual thinking. These definitions make the connection necessary to understand the development of the strategic concepts needed when planning for the future of an organization.

A leader who does not have a strategic vision in place oftentimes hinders movement toward the future for an organization. Nonprofits are notorious for not having a strategic plan in place. Churches especially fail to plan for crisis. They are excellent at making the vision plain and communicating that vision with passion, but they often fail to set in place a strategic vision. As servant-leaders, we must have vision.

Going back to the biblical principles of vision, Proverbs 29:18 states, "Where there is no vision, the people perish." And Habakkuk 2:2 instructs us to make it plain. The great biblical strategist, Nehemiah, established and worked through a well-planned strategy to accomplish the vision God had given him to rebuild the walls of Jerusalem. Therefore, as Christian leaders, God has instructed us to plan for the future. And when we do not lead the church with a strategic plan, we are not following God's Word.

Visual Leadership

Strategic planning for the future requires an understanding of the "two distinct but related types of leadership at play: transactional and transformational."[17] We discussed these types of leaders earlier and see them in future pages as they play an important role in servant-leadership coaching.

Transactional leadership is an exchange process between leaders and followers in which they "focus on the present and excel at keeping the organization running smoothly and efficiently. Transformational leaders have the ability to lead changes in the organization's vision, strategy, and culture."[18]

While organizations need traits of both these types of leaders, the transformational leader is the one to lead the organization into the future through the use of strategic thinking, which will give the people of an organization a direction to work toward. This is not to say a person cannot possess the traits of both a transactional and transformational leader. A third type of leadership that important to this model of coaching is the servant-leader.

Understand, leadership is not something that is done to people, but it occurs among them. Great leaders "anticipate where change is going and make sure their organizations get there first."[19] They know their organizations, the core competencies, the vision, and the mission and understand the need to "influence change as it is emerging."[20] The relationships leaders build create the foundation needed to survive and move forward in a world of change. The foundations created by these relationships hold the organization up in the future. Strategic thinking and planning are future-oriented tasks. Therefore, let's look at leadership studies and how to lead followers into the future.

Visual Thinking Leaders Create Vision Strategy

In today's complex global environment, unpredictable changes, time, and uncertainty play an important role in carrying out the vision. As global borders shrink, so many establishments, including churches, nonprofit charitable organizations, and service-oriented businesses, are becoming multiracial, multiethnic organizations that have to think in terms of global complexity. Considering current changes in the world, many associations have been forced from the competition arena and predictions about the future have failed,[21] giving time and uncertainty an important role in the strategic planning process.

Organizations try to identify, strengthen, and improve their capabilities for adapting and improving their knowledge and skills to cope with turbulent environments. They do this while in a complex and competitive environment saturated by compact markets. Lacking strategic planning, the organization is placed in a poor competitive situation that eventually causes them to confront failure. Therefore, if an industry such as the church wants to compete with worldly influences, adapting itself to external environments and member needs, it must develop a strategy through planning. The same holds true for nonprofit organizations and service-oriented organizations such as the medical field.

Richard Daft defined strategy in *The Leadership Experience* as "a general plan of action that describes resource allocation and other activities for dealing with the environment and helping the organization realize its goals."[22] In other words, if the leadership does not have a plan of action in place for allocating resources, they have no method of leading when the resources are depleting.

We are not only looking to someone in charge, we are looking to those people who have built a relationship of influence where "leaders are change agents engaged in furthering the needs, wants, and goals of leaders and followers alike."[23] Keeping these two definitions in mind, we can see that strategic leaders are change agents who have a relationship with followers and work to create a plan of action for the organization to succeed within its environment, always striving for the vision set before the people.

Coaching the Vision

The process of coaching stimulates vision development and moving people forward. Using the servant-leadership coaching model, the coach helps leaders clarify the present, get in touch with their circumstances, know themselves, and find the passion that drives them toward the goal.[24] Servant-leadership coaching can help a team or an individual achieve greater clarity of vision or purpose and increase self-awareness. This is a critical element and a key characteristic of leadership excellence.[25] Encouraging vision development and clarification is one step toward developing the leader to be more of a servant-leader. Vision is an integral part of coaching as it provides an image of "how we can get from where we are not to where we can and believe we should be."[26]

Summary

Everyone needs a road map to know where he or she is headed and how not to get lost. That road map also shows how to get back on track. In organizations as well as our personal life, that road map is our vision of where we want to go and how we plan to get there. "Visions inspire and visionary leaders attract followers because both capture the imagination and excite people to anticipate dreams that are possible to achieve."[27] It is the multitool of the modern organization.

Casting vision and inciting excitement is leadership's job. Through excitement, the members take ownership and understand why things are the way they are. They better accept the ways of the organization when they know where the organization is headed. Vision is the important piece of the puzzle to get the organization where it needs to be. Through strategic planning, the organization can move seamlessly through the twists and turns of growth and wind up at their goal.

The purpose of strategic thinking is to create a strategy that is a coherent, unifying, integrative framework for decisions, especially about the direction of the organization and the use of resources. Strategic thinking uses internal and external data and a qualitative mixture of opinions and perceptions. It is conscious, explicit, and proactive and defines the competitive sphere for organizational strategic advantage. The strategy is a key outcome of a relevant strategic-thinking process.

Strategy must be comprehensive, yet it can be simple. It "is about making choices" and acting on those choices while "still trusting your instincts."[28] Leaders should study the present, looking for patterns and direction on which to envision the future. They then shape that future through their choices and actions and establish plans to create success and facilitate crisis management.

Servant-leadership coaching utilizes tools to help the leader create the vision, communicate the vision, and implement the vision while meeting the needs of the followers and meeting the goals of the organization. All Christian leaders should engage in God-ordained strategic thinking and planning. Proverbs 21:5 advises, "The plans of the diligent lead to profit as surely as haste leads to poverty."

8

Facilitating Change While Being Accessible

Give whatever you are doing and whoever you are with the gift of your attention.

—Jim Rohn

As we begin to talk about being accessible, think about what *accessible* means to you. For most of us, the word *accessible* means that something is available to us or within reach, such as buildings being handicap accessible, computers having access to the Internet, or having coffee or water accessible to our customers, clients, or employees. But do we ever consider ourselves accessible to other people?

The age of technology has taken over our lives to the point that in many areas we are living a half-truth. I don't want to say a lie, because it is partially true, but I will call it a half-truth. Because of the affordability of the cell phone and Internet, almost everyone is accessible to others twenty-four hours a day, seven days a week. We boast of how accessible we are because we always have our phone on us, and our Internet is always on. And, of course, with the smartphone technology, we do not even need a computer to be accessible by e-mail or social media. All the messages come straight to our phones; people are virtually connected all the time.[1] We can access any information any time with the click of the screen, and that includes reaching other people to talk to, message, or post about. But is this true accessibility? And how accessible do we want to be? What about when we don't want to be bothered? All we have to do is ignore a message, a call, or post. So actually, we are accessible, we are reachable.

Literally every day, information and communication technology teams are seeking new means and tools to reach out to tech-savvy target audiences with promises of becoming more accessible to the world and the world becoming more accessible to them.[2] There is a true difference between being reachable and being accessible. When I am accessible, you can reach me any time you need me and get something out of me. It may not be exactly what you were looking for, but it will still be an answer of some sort to the issue you have. When I am reachable, you can reach out and send me a message. I will receive that message, but you may not get any answer as I may choose to ignore the message. Leaders must be not only reachable but accessible to be effective leaders. True servant-leaders are accessible to

Changed Mind, Changed Heart

those following them as they work to transform lives and transform their organizations.

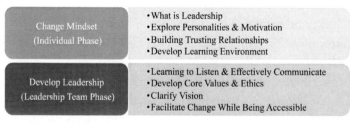

Figure 16. Servant-Leadership Coaching Model, Stage 2, Phase 4.

In forging forward through the servant-leadership coaching model, the final step in developing the leader is facilitating change while being accessible. Change is difficult by itself, but by developing the leader into a servant-leader who walks the journey of change with the followers of the organization, change can be manageable, even successful. The ICF core competency four is "coaching presence—ability to be fully conscious and create spontaneous relationship with the client, employing a style that is open, flexible and confident."[3] This shows the importance of accessibility in the coaching process.

The Importance of Accessibility

Being accessible to followers is important to begin building trust and show that you truly care. "One of the most significant ways in which you can show others that you care and appreciate others' efforts is to be out there with them."[4]

People want to know you care enough about them to get to know them. It is important as a leader to build trusting relationships with people. One way to do that is to be open, honest, and available to them. Being accessible makes the leader more genuine, approachable, and human. Successful leaders are accessible and ask for input.

In 2007, aftermarketbusiness.com published a segment on "becoming a user-friendly leader" in which they described leaders who are accessible, help with problem-solving, work alongside employees, laugh with followers, build great relationships, are authentic in who they are, get to know their employees and volunteers, and add value to the people around them.[5]

Looking at this list of traits, we see a true servant-leader's heart. These traits add up to leaders who care about their employees and volunteers and show that care through their actions, putting followers' needs first.

Being accessible opens doors of opportunity for people to open up, it "leads to innovation as well as creating solutions to issues from the mundane to the complex."[6] When people feel you care about them and what they know, they reveal their ideas, creating solutions and innovations for the future. If you are not accessible, keeping to yourself for whatever reason, it communicates to other people that you do not need their help or value their help. Open communication opens the lines to accessibility and removes misconstrued ideas about how people feel.

Levels of Accessibility According to Leadership Style

Different leadership styles call for different accessibility to the follower. We previously discussed the styles of transactional leaders, transformational leaders, and servant-leaders. Let's look at these three styles from the point of view of being accessible.

Transactional Leader

Transactional leadership is based on expectations both of the leader and the follower. The leader gives the follower something the follower wants in exchange for something the leader wants, creating a mutual dependence in which the contributions of both sides are acknowledged and rewarded. Because of this mutual dependence, the leader becomes more influential because doing what the leader expects is in the best interest of the follower.

In addition, effective transactional leaders must regularly fulfill the expectations of their followers, making the outcome contingent on leaders' abilities to meet and respond to the reactions and changing expectations of their followers. In other words, transactional leadership represents those exchanges in which both the superior and the subordinate influence one another reciprocally so that each derives something of value.[7]

Understanding the value and methods of the transactional leader, we can see how accessibility is not a first concern of this type of leadership style. Accessibility would come into play in the process of ascertaining what the follower wants or needs in return for the task to be performed. However, there could be cases where accessibility to the leader is the reward for completion of a task to the leader's expectations. Part of the problem could be the growth of organizations in the world today. With them growing larger and larger, the senior transactional leaders unfortunately are being moved farther away from the people. That makes accessibility and interaction with employees more difficult, even though it is more important today than ever.[8]

Transformational Leader

The transformational leader is all about change, whether individual or organizational. A "key behavior of successful transformational leaders may include articulating goals, building an image, demonstrating confidence, and arousing motivation."[9] Transformational leaders operate out of deeply held personal values, including justice and integrity, which cannot be negotiated or exchanged between individuals.[10]

When expressing these personal standards, the result oftentimes is the ability for the transformational leader to unite followers and to change followers' goals and beliefs. "The result of transforming leadership is a relationship of mutual stimulation and elevation that converts followers into leaders and may convert leaders into moral agents"[11]

The transformational leader's level of accessibility and approachableness is higher than that of the transactional leader. The transformational leader is more open and available to followers in order to effectuate change, but there is still an element of looking out for the interest of the leader or organization above all else. The transformational leader typically achieves results of change for the good of the organization by his or her influence on the follower. This influence is gained by demonstrating important personal characteristics.

Servant-Leader

Servant-leadership is a long-term transformational approach to both life and work. The term servant-leadership, coined in 1970 by Greenleaf, merges the role of servant and leader into one person. Greenleaf believed that more servants should emerge as leaders. Servant-leaders approach tasks with an understanding of the roles and values of the organization. They are concerned with mutual trust and a desire to shift from self-interest to service. They are willing to be influenced by others, welcome new experiences and challenges, and see change as an opportunity for growth.[12]

Accessibility requires communication. When communication is kept open and honest, it likely will increase the effectiveness of the organization and the relationships that are built on mutual trust. Feedback from both leader and follower is an appropriate behavior in servant-leadership, which is rarely found in the other styles of leadership. When we look at the characteristics of servant-leadership—listening, empathy, healing, awareness, persuasion, conceptualization, foresight, stewardship, commitment to people's development, and building community—we can better understand how accessibility is a key trait of the servant-leader. The sole interest of the servant-leader is to develop those they lead, which requires being available and interested in what they want to say.

Change, Accessibility, and the Servant-Leader

The servant-leader takes on the challenge of exposing different worldviews in his or her followers. When done correctly, the servant-leadership approach opens the opportunity for creating a positive change throughout the organization, community, and world.[13] This change is effective through servant-leadership practices of accessibility.

- The leader values people through believing in people by placing others' needs before his own through receptive, nonjudgmental listening.
- The leader develops people by providing opportunities for learning and growth.
- The leader role-models appropriate behaviors.
- The leader values and respects others' differences.

- At all times, the leader displays authenticity.
- The leader provides leadership by envisioning the future, taking initiative and clarifying goals.
- The leader shares leadership by facilitating a shared vision; he shares power and releases control.[14]

The servant-leader's approach still demands a motivation to lead while requiring the leader to want to serve the organization and its people. In being supportive and encouraging, the servant-leadership approach empowers people around him. Servant-leadership requires the leader to facilitate the success of his team by thinking and asking "what can I do for my team?" "what obstacles can I remove for them to achieve their organizational goals?" The servant-leader works within an organization that is committed to building a learning organization in which individuals are encouraged to grow and express their unique value.

Practicing principles of servant-leadership not only creates change in the workplace or home but also around the world. By creating, growing, and empowering people through servant-leadership, we see overall growth of the organization.[15] When we are accessible to others and follow servant-leadership principles, followers are invited to participate in a more team-oriented approach rather than being viewed as assets of the organization. There are two types of leadership accessibility.

Active Leadership Accessibility

In practicing active leadership accessibility, the leader purposely seeks employees to engage in conversations, learning who they are and their challenges, needs, and perspectives of what is going on in their work unit and obtaining ideas for the organization from them.[16] The follower—employee, volunteer, member, and client—does not have to schedule a time to see and talk to the leader as the leader should be the one initiating the meeting. These types of impromptu meetings make the leader more relational and aid in the growth of the follower and organization.

Much can be learned about the workings of the organization from these short impromptu meetings, such as how employees feel about their job, organizational goals, and needs of the organization or employees.[17] Followers feel they can better talk with the leader. A deeper trust and relationship are built, and the human side of the leader is seen by all.

Passive Leadership Accessibility

Passive leadership accessibility places the responsibility on employees to seek leaders through a typical open-door policy. Therefore, it is in some ways easier than active leadership accessibility.[18] This is more of an open-door form of leadership. Followers can seek the leader when they have a concern or question, which might make the leader feel like he or she has more time to devote to other tasks. However, there are significant trade-offs that make the least effective accessibility effort.

Most people will not take advantage of an open-door policy unless they need to discuss something incredibly serious. This means you will not be hearing about a majority of the questions, complaints, or ideas—factors that could really impact your organization. You take the chance of only hearing about an issue once it has become a crisis! The leader might miss out on the positive benefits of active leadership accessibility, including not taking advantage of the collaborative efforts of actively seeking employees and getting their counsel on developing policies, procedures, or new ideas.[19]

There is a time and place for both forms of accessibility, and the servant-leader will utilize both depending on the situation. An open-door policy is not feasible in large organizations, which makes it difficult on leaders. If they are unable to communicate and solve problems with their teams, they are not personally effective. People skills and accessibility are critical to leadership because they are a major part of building trust. Without trust, it is nearly impossible to move forward.[20]

As you grow into a more successful, accessible servant-leader, more demands are made for your time. Your time is divided among an increasing number of people. When you give your time to one person or activity, you are also taking available time away from other people and activities. You only have so many hours in a day. Leadership accessibility becomes a delicate balancing act. However, you must have some level of accessibility if you are to be an effective leader because people need you.

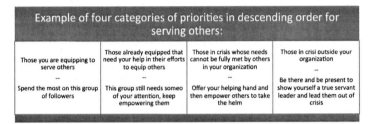

Figure 17. Serving Categories.

Characteristics of an Accessible Leader

Accessible leaders are *communicators*. They know how to talk to people to help them see the good in what they are doing. They empower others through their communication, have excellent listening skills, and are present in the conversation with the follower. The accessible leader's nonverbal communication exhibits care and value for what the speaker says. They have a passion and focus to recognize all attempts to communicate with them.

Accessible leaders are *responders*, responding to followers communicating with them. They respond to every voice mail, e-mail, and text even if it is late at night or early the next morning. They are driven by the need felt for their advice on the subject, which is one reason they are so quick to respond and driven to respond to everyone. Responding to communication shows followers they are valued by the leader.

Accessible leaders love people and, therefore, are usually the most *visible* leaders. They are often cornered for long periods of time by individuals wanting to speak to them regardless of where they are because they are so attentive and positive. They are approachable yet still have boundaries.

Coaching Change Accessibility

Coaching is all about change, it empowers people to reach new levels. Coaching helps organizations to change the way they perform and treat stakeholders. It is about developing vision and setting goals. "When coaching is successful, it's about bringing and maintaining change."[21] Coaches are change agents. They help people see what and where they need to change and what they need to leave unchanged. The servant-leadership coaching model is about helping the leader to develop into a servant-leader, making the changes necessary to meet the needs of others while reaching organizational goals.

In order to be a change agent in developing the leader, the coach must encourage the leader to practice active leadership accessibility as discussed earlier in the chapter. Through active leadership accessibility, the leader makes a point to go to followers and learn what needs they have, what would make their job better, help them serve the customer better, and discover how to serve the members of a church or nonprofit organization better.[22] The active accessible leader is about meeting the needs of the stakeholder, regardless of what title you put on that follower—employee, volunteer, church member, patient, or client.

In addition to encouraging the leader to be an accessible leader, coaches must be accessible. Modeling a behavior is one way to teach and guide others. The coach models the behavior. The leader makes necessary changes and models behavior of accessibility to followers. In turn, followers begin to exhibit the same behavior. The organization then becomes one of servant-leadership, taking care of the needs of others while meeting the goals of the organization, one of which should be serving others.

Summary

How do you become an accessible servant-leader? Rethink the paradigm of leadership and search your own heart as a leader. Are you doing what you love doing? Is there more to what you want to accomplish? Are your followers your main concern, or is your success as leader the main focus in your work? These are questions leaders must ask themselves when becoming a servant-leader who is fully accessible. Give this some thought to see if your personal aspirations and growth strategies may be short-circuiting the pursuit of your leadership accessibility.

Being the leader of an organization is not intended to be a one-person show. You need other leaders, followers, customers, clients, and members. You need people. Think back to chapter 2 when we discussed relationships. Human beings need relationship. The world is a better place when those relationships are built on trust and care for others above our own needs. Where we have moved off-kilter and become a society of *me* leaders, I do not know. But I know that when we start acting like servant-leaders, empowering others and growing followers, no longer worried about them surpassing us, we will see growth and change in our organizations.

Servant-leadership coaching encourages changing the organization from having passive accessible leadership to one where active leadership accessibility is prevalent. This is done through understanding what it means to be accessible, changing behaviors, and modeling the behaviors you want to prevail within your organization.

Be kind, personable, and compassionate, not only on the surface, but in the heart. Leaders who lead with heart and are authentic and honest not only lead but grow. Being accessible has everything to do with how we express ourselves outwardly, being genuinely kind and gracious. Let people know you want to help and that you are there for them. Meet with them. Talk with them. Listen to them. It is an excellent way to cultivate accessibility and improve your leadership. But most of all, be there and show someone you care.

Part III

Cultivate the Culture to Make Enduring Changes

Culture is the process by which a person becomes all that they were created capable of being.

—Thomas Carlyle

9

Inspiring Others Through Empowerment

How wonderful it is that nobody need wait a single moment before starting to improve the world.

—Anne Frank

Carl was a quiet man. He didn't talk much. He would always greet you with a big smile and a firm handshake. Even after living in our neighborhood for over 50 years, no one could really say they knew him very well. Before his retirement, he took the bus to work each morning. The lone sight of him walking down the street often worried us. He had a slight limp from a bullet wound received in WWII. Watching him, we worried that although he had survived WWII, he may not make it through our changing uptown neighborhood with its ever-increasing random violence, gangs, and drug activity. When he saw the flyer at our local church asking for volunteers for caring for the gardens behind the minister's residence, he responded in his characteristically unassuming manner. Without fanfare, he just signed up. He was well into his 87th year when the very thing we had always feared finally happened. He was just finishing his watering for the day when three gang members approached him. Ignoring their attempt to intimidate him, he simply asked, "Would you like a drink from the hose?" The tallest and toughest-looking of the three said, "Yeah, sure," with a malevolent little smile. As Carl offered the hose to him, the other two grabbed Carl's arm, throwing him down. As the hose snaked crazily over the ground, dousing everything in its way, Carl's assailants stole his retirement watch and his wallet, and then fled. Carl tried to get himself up, but he had been thrown down on his bad leg. He lay there trying to gather himself as the minister came running to help him. Although the minister had witnessed the attack from his window, he couldn't get there fast enough to stop it. "Carl, are you okay? Are you hurt?" the minister kept asking as he helped Carl to his feet. Carl just passed a hand over his brow and sighed, shaking his head. "Just some punk kids. I hope they'll wise-up someday." His wet clothes clung to his slight frame as he bent to pick up the hose. He adjusted the nozzle again and started to water. Confused and a little concerned, the minister asked, "Carl, what are you doing?" "I've got to finish my watering. It's been very dry lately," came the calm reply. Satisfying himself that Carl really was all right,

Changed Mind, Changed Heart

the minister could only marvel. Carl was a man from a different time and place. A few weeks later the three returned. Just as before their threat was unchallenged. Carl again offered them a drink from his hose. This time they didn't rob him. They wrenched the hose from his hand and drenched him head to foot in the icy water. When they had finished their humiliation of him, they sauntered off down the street, throwing catcalls and curses, falling over one another laughing at the hilarity of what they had just done. Carl just watched them. Then he turned toward the warmth giving sun, picked up his hose, and went on with his watering. The summer was quickly fading into fall Carl was doing some tilling when he was startled by the sudden approach of someone behind him. He stumbled and fell into some evergreen branches. As he struggled to regain his footing, he turned to see the tall leader of his summer tormentors reaching down for him. He braced himself for the expected attack. "Don't worry old man, I'm not gonna hurt you this time." The young man spoke softly, still offering the tattooed and scarred hand to Carl. As he helped Carl get up, the man pulled a crumpled bag from his pocket and handed it to Carl. "What's this?" Carl asked. It's your stuff," the man explained. "It's your stuff back. Even the money in your wallet" "I don't understand," Carl said. "Why would you help me now?" The man shifted his feet, seeming embarrassed and ill at ease. "I learned something from you," he said. "I ran with that gang and hurt people like you. We picked you because you were old and we knew we could do it. But every time we came and did something to you, instead of yelling and fighting back, you tried to give us a drink. You didn't hate us for hating you. You kept showing love against our hate." He stopped for a moment. "I couldn't sleep after we stole your stuff, so here it is back." He paused for another awkward moment, not knowing what more there was to say. "That bag's my way of saying thanks for straightening me out, I guess." And with that, he walked off down the street. Carl looked down at the sack in his hands and gingerly opened it. He took out his retirement watch and put it back on his wrist. Opening his wallet, he checked for his wedding photo. He gazed for a moment at the young bride that still smiled back at him from all those years ago. He died one cold day after Christmas that winter. Many people attended his funeral in spite of the weather. In particular the minister noticed a tall young man that he didn't know sitting quietly in a distant corner of the church. The minister spoke of Carl's garden as a lesson in life. In a voice made thick with unshed tears, he said, "Do your best and make your garden as beautiful as you can. We will never forget Carl and his garden." The following spring another flyer went up. It read: "Person needed to care for Carl's garden." The flyer went unnoticed by the busy parishioners until one day when a knock was heard at the minister's office door. Opening the door, the minister saw a pair of scarred and tattooed hands holding the flyer. "I believe this is my job, if you'll have me," the young man said. The minister recognized him as the same young man who had returned the stolen watch and wallet to Carl. He knew that Carl's kindness had turned this man's life around. As the minister handed him the keys to the garden shed, he said, "Yes, go take care of Carl's garden and honor him." The man went to work and, over the next several years, he tended the flowers and vegetables just as Carl had done. During that time, he went to college, got married, and became a prominent member of the community. But he never forgot his promise to Carl's memory and kept the garden as beautiful as he thought Carl would have kept it. One day he approached the new minister and told him that he couldn't care for the garden any longer. He explained with a shy and happy smile, "My wife just had a baby boy last night, and she's bringing him home on Saturday." "Well, congratulations!" said the minister, as he was handed the garden shed keys. "That's wonderful! What's the baby's name?" "Carl," he replied."[1]

This story touches the heart in so many areas. The area that appealed to me the most is that without setting out to make a difference, just being himself, Carl made an enormous impact on this young man's life. Carl empowered him to become a pillar of the community by being kind and not showing hatred when, by all rights, he should have. Carl empowered this young man through his life, through his inspiration, and through his wisdom of seeing the good in people.

There are times in our lives when we need little encouragement. Sometimes that encouragement comes silently from someone we meet, like Carl. Other times, it is intentional. But the bottom line is that it is through simply believing in someone that people inspire others to go on to do greater things. That is what inspiring others through empowerment and servant-leadership is about.

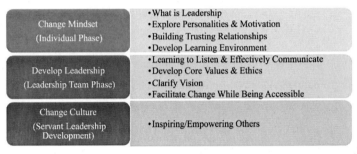

Figure 18. Servant-Leadership Coaching Model, Stage 3, Phase 1.

The final phase of the servant-leadership coaching model is to cultivate the culture to make enduring changes. The first step in this process is to inspire others through empowerment. After we have changed the mind-set and developed the leaders, the culture of the organization will begin to see changes. By becoming a culture of inspiring and empowering others, we set them on the course for greatness.

Servant-Leadership Empowers

In focusing on the interests of followers and the organization over their own personal interest, leaders facilitate a mutual sharing of responsibility and power with followers. When they include the follower's feedback in developing the vision, it is more likely the follower will perceive the leader's culture as servant-oriented and mimic that leadership style.[2] We see this servant orientation through valuing and developing people, building relational and authentic community, and providing and sharing leadership.

Servant-leadership is refraining from using power, influence, and position to advance oneself but is rather to empower, enable, and encourage those within one's circle of influence.[3] The servant-leader uses a variety of inputs in the decision-making process, considering every employee, volunteer, and customer as a source of knowledge, echoing the importance of communication and empowerment in servant-leadership. When we look at the leadership role in the servant-leadership model, we see the concern for growth of people, providing encouragement and teaching,[4] and helping followers to grow and succeed.[5] The greater the congruence between the values of leaders and followers, the more effective the leader should be.

Leaders talk about their initiatives, targets, and mission statements, but while doing so, not all possess a vision and sense of service to the community. It is important to introduce staff to some sort of direction, a shared vision that will bring them all together using essential components of culture such as core values, stories, rites, and rituals. Ethical leaders influence the organization and its member to incorporate and exhibit desirable virtues and behaviors.[6]

While the concept of empowerment is closely aligned with propulsion to gain organizational effectiveness through the wise utilization of human resources, care should be given as to how we treat and empower individuals.[7] Positive environments, paralleled with a servant-oriented culture, nurtures the productivity of members, followers, and leaders, thereby empowering them to be all they can be.[8]

According to Greenleaf, servant-leaders are characterized by two distinct stages of empowering their followers, as opposed to the organization as a whole. He contended they serve the needs of the follower to empower them to achieve their potential and aspire and mature them into leading.[9] A true servant-leader helps others grow and live through a new paradigm, one with risk and responsibility, making his or her follower independent. This is accomplished through modeling and teaching. In modeling, you are showing you care; in teaching, you are empowering.

In order to do this, mental, physical, emotional, and spiritual tools are needed. Our strengths are what define us, our weaknesses are our insufficiently developed strengths, and our esteem allows us to recognize our strengths. One of the largest needs among humans is greater self-esteem.

Changing the pyramid, servant-leaders put the team at the top. Instead of making all the decisions on their own, servant-leaders look to their team to provide feedback and challenge their ideas.[10]

By empowering the follower in this manner, a bond is created. The follower takes ownership in the organization, and there is a greater connection between leader and follower, and more productivity in reaching the organization's goals. The leader at the top of the pyramid still makes all the decisions but with the help of the team, facilitating cohesiveness.

Coaching Leaders to Empower Followers

Developing the skills of the leader and follower requires training, education, new assignments, and promotion. The ability to coach the follower is an important asset for the leader to possess. Being coached in a leader development program will teach leaders how to coach others, encouraging clients to draw on the power they have within them to accomplish what they seek to achieve.[11]

Coaching is a noncontrolling aspect of leadership. When leaders are too controlling, they block the potential talents and intelligence of followers, not utilizing them to their fullest potential. "People cannot take risks unless they feel safe, unless they feel secure that they will not be unfairly treated, embarrassed, harassed, or harmed by taking action. When we feel safe we become more open to outside influences and learning."[12] Servant-leaders aim to unleash the maximum amount of contribution each individual can bring to the organization.

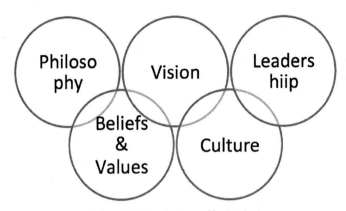

Figure 19. Contribution of Individuals.

Utilizing philosophy, beliefs and values, vision, culture, and leadership, the leaders of an organization, through coaching, can unleash the potential in others and add value to the organization. Inspiring the follower through training of the behaviors, expectations, beliefs, and values that direct the leaders decisions, followers not only learn how to lead, they excel at leading.[13]

Culture is a prominent factor in the differences people experience and can be critical in effectively managing organizational diversity. Culture motivates employees: "it is the culture leaders create, nurture, and sustain that will most affect their people."[14] Culture determines how people

Changed Mind, Changed Heart

do things and how well they do them. If the culture is in line with the goals of the organization, people perform to their maximum potential, and the overall success of the organization reflects this. By creating a culture for growth, development, and performance, leaders set the tone to achieve.

Another reason culture is important is because shared values tend to regularize human behavior and make individuals more predictable. Knowing how others perceive and value their environment provides a guide for leaders to anticipate behavior and respond effectively. This point is becoming increasingly more important as globalization brings distant peoples into closer contact as they face cultural, economic, and legal challenges.

The growth in international trade has dramatically increased people's understanding of the similarities and differences between diverse cultures. Service-oriented public and private administrators must become effective managers of individuals with diverse cultures, backgrounds, and interests.[15] According to John Maxwell, "Cross-cultural connecting requires a lot of mental, physical, and emotional energy."[16]

In today's competitive world, understanding and responding to culturally driven behaviors are paramount to succeeding in cross-cultural management because "the people in an organization are crucial to its performance and the quality of work life within it."[17] Traditionally, both

India and Afghanistan are collective and high-context cultures where women often stay home and are responsible for rearing children, while men work outside of the house.

However, women are playing bigger roles in the workforce of both these countries. There has been a paradigm shift where women are encouraged to go out and work. In Afghanistan, both men and women work inside and outside of their home to help support their family. "Contrary to popular views in the west, many Afghan men oppose traditional ideologies of male superiority and dominance."[18] Women in India are also becoming more accepted in the workforce due to economic reforms.

> While social, legal, and economic reforms have helped women to join the workforce in India, the continuing influence of normative attitudes and values have prevented them from altering the perceptions of the society as well as their own regarding their sex-roles.[19]

Changes in the global economy have introduced new gender roles that have made organizations more diverse and full of managers with different managerial skills and propensities.

Understanding these global changes and the cultural needs of followers puts the servant-leader in a better position to meet needs and empower followers for greatness. Oftentimes, we seem to believe our way of thinking and doing is the only right way, without regard to other cultural norms. Forcing our way on others can create frustration, panic, and tension. Instead, we should inspire every member of the organization to take positive actions to demonstrate a commitment built on their individual talents,[20] empowering them to help take the organization to new levels or productivity and success.

Understanding how others think and utilizing their talents can remove the stress of change. A true servant-leader who is seeking to put the needs of the follower before his or her own will explore the follower's culture and adapt the organizational culture with a happy medium.

One such way to adapt is through education and coaching for both followers and leaders. When leaders are educated to the cultural norms of the follower, they can make necessary changes in the way they lead to incorporate some of the cultural norms of the follower. This would empower followers by giving them a sense of belonging and ownership in the organization. Similarly, educating followers can bring a smoother flow into operation when followers know what is expected of them, how the organization is formed, and what the foundational beliefs are for all involved.

Summary

In anticipating the future, leaders are preparing for the unknown. By creating a plan, leaders have a strategy for recognizing opportunity. In living the vision, communicating it, and acting it, leaders demonstrate their vision through their actions as opposed to simply stating it.

To create an environment that encourages personal growth, a few factors are essential: visibly valuing the contributions of others, sincerely and frequently; being receptive to learning from others; encouraging others to own their responsibilities; giving feedback frequently, both positive and negative; creating win-win solutions; and practicing empathy.[21]

Education on cultural norms and beliefs is an important segment of empowering others. Everyone is different. Everyone has different belief systems and value systems. To bring that diversity together, working together will create a successful organization. Taking the time to learn about diversity and culture will show the follower that, as the leader of the organization, you care and they matter to you as a person, not just an asset. People want to know they are cared about.

By learning about them and adapting to some of their ways, we show they matter, thereby increasing their productivity. Cultural diversity is no longer a possibility, it is a reality.[22] We are seeing more and more cultural diversity in our workplaces, worship centers, and our world. We must embrace cultural diversity to successfully work and do business.

To advocate for positive change, one must accept it, embrace it, and even initiate it.[23] Some followers may be fearful of change. For that reason, the leader must show how change is an opportunity to grow, increase satisfaction in both employee and customer, and contribute to the overall success of the organization. Integrating results and relationships refers to a leader's priority to honor *performance* alludes in addition to the *people* values.

Remember, leadership is a combination of your character (who you are) and your skills and competence (the things you do). Servant-leaders enable others to grow, as opposed to doing their jobs for them. Encourage your future leaders to choose to make a difference and coach them to pay encouragement forward. Inspire your followers and customers to become all they can become.

10

Supporting the Community Through Cultural Awareness

The greatest gift that you can give to others is the gift of unconditional love and acceptance.

—Brian Tracy

An elderly woman and her little grandson, whose face was sprinkled with bright freckles, spent the day at the zoo. Lots of children were waiting in line to get their cheeks painted by a local artist who was decorating them with tiger paws. "You've got so many freckles, there's no place to paint!" a girl in the line said to the little fella. Embarrassed, the little boy dropped his head. His grandmother knelt down next to him. "I love your freckles. When I was a little girl I always wanted freckles," she said, while tracing her finger across the child's cheek. "Freckles are beautiful." The boy looked up, "Really?" "Of course," said the grandmother. "Why just name me one thing that's prettier than freckles." The little boy thought for a moment, peered intensely into his grandma's face and softly whispered, "Wrinkles." (Author unknown)

This story teaches such an elementary lesson that we all seem to fail at one time or another. We hear on the news that intolerance of others is becoming commonplace. Why? Why do we behave in such a way? This little boy found something that would cause many his age to shy away from his grandmother instead of to focus on and accept her for.

Too often we want to tell people what is and is not acceptable. We try to show them the right way to do things. We believe our way is superior, instead of accepting others for who they are. We always want to change others rather than celebrate their differences. If we stop and think for a moment, their differences could just be the very thing that excels our organization. Instead, we stop our own progress by not accepting another way. Supporting the community through acceptance is just that—accepting a different way of doing things.

Figure 20. Servant-Leadership Coaching Model, Stage 3, Phase 2.

The next step in the servant-leadership coaching model is supporting community. To support community, we need to concentrate on culture and cultural differences to understand why we do the things we do, and why we should accept other behaviors within our organizational borders.

What's the Big Deal About Culture?

Culture is an elusive, conceptual design that shapes everything we do.[1]

Defining culture is much like defining air. We know what it is. We live in it. It lives in us. We can't see it, but it's there just the same. And like air, technical definitions of culture abound, but they don't necessarily move us any closer toward understanding what it really is and how it affects us.[2]

We live in culture every day. It is considered the anthropologist's label for the sum of distinctive characteristics of a community, region, or nation's way of life. It is more than language, dress, and food customs. Culture "is the conceptual design, the definitions by which people order their lives, interpret their experiences, and evaluate the behavior of others."[3]

Culture has also been described metaphorically as an iceberg. One can see the artifacts in culture, such as foods, eating habits, gestures, music, economic practices, dress, use of physical space, worship, art, and more. However, that is only the portion of culture we can see. Looking below the surface to see the most significant aspects of culture is the challenge.[4]

Cultural groups share race, ethnicity, and nationality, but people fail to comprehend that a cultural group also arises from segments of generation, socioeconomic class, sexual orientation, ability and disability, political and religious affiliation, language, and gender. Even though human behavior occurs within particular cultures, within socially defined contexts,[5] it is important to remember that cultures are always changing. Furthermore, they relate to the symbolic dimension of life or the place where we are constantly making meaning and enacting our identities.

Culture is learned and shared one with another in a process whereby people perceive and respond to one another in culturally conditioned ways.

> Most of culture lies hidden and is outside voluntary control, making up the warp and weft of human existence. It penetrates to the roots of an individual's nervous system and determines how he perceives the world. Even when small fragments of culture are elevated to awareness, they are difficult to change.[6]

David Livermore gave us three subculture domains on which to build all cultures: socioethnic, organizational, and generational.

Socioethnic Culture

Socioethnic culture is a broad and elusive domain because it includes national cultures. A national culture is such as the one shared by everyone who lives in the United States. Numerous ethnic cultures exist within the United States: various African-American, Asian-American, Hispanic-American, and European-American cultures. These socioethnic cultures are made up of personal cultures that are unique to each individual. These personal cultures are "the combination of (1) the personal cultural heritage acquired through socialization with our parents, (2) the broader cultural heritage acquired through enculturation and feedback from the community, and (3) our act of accepting or rejecting those forces."[7]

We see cultural differences that are much more obvious when we move across national boundaries than what we experience when we interact cross-culturally within our own national culture. However, there is a greater challenge to being effective across national boundaries than it is to do so closer to home. A big challenge in moving across national cultures is that we may see artifacts that resemble what we see in our own culture; however, they might mean something completely different.[8]

Organizational Culture

In evaluating organizational culture, we find that organizations like countries and socioethnic groups have a *shared personality*. Similar to socioethnic culture, organizations have artifacts that provide us with cues about what is valued and assumed. An example of these artifacts would be furniture arrangement in an office; the organization's heroes, both internally and externally; what members wear; and what they brag about, all of which says something about the leadership that runs the organization.[9] Effective leadership requires a growing understanding of the powerful values and assumptions that drive the organizations to which we belong.

Organizational culture can be sliced up and applied in a variety of ways. The organizational culture in which you work is likely comprised of numerous subcultures. One of the challenges of leadership is to grow in understanding of which organizational culture most strongly affects how they serve, compete, and communicate.[10]

Generational Culture

Generational cultures cover not only age subcultures of individuals but also generational eras. The subculture of each age or era is usually different in significant ways from that of the generation preceding it. There are many ways to categorize generational cultures that exist. Some of the familiar ways are as the builders or traditionalist, the boomers or moderns, Generation X, and Generation Y.

Employing cultural intelligence (CQ) within a specific organization provides the opportunity to interact with people in one's own geographic context who come from different socioethnic, organizational, or generational backgrounds. This interaction leads to acceptance and development of a culturally diverse organization. Servant-leadership coaching promotes this acceptance, accepting all people for who they are and empowering followers through that acceptance.

Cultural Intelligence

The CQ quotient measures one's ability to effectively reach across the chasm of cultural difference in ways that are loving and respectful. Becoming culturally intelligent is the beginning to becoming more aware of one's own cultural identity, which includes the varied cultural domains—socioethnic culture, organizational culture, and generational culture. Ignoring the reality of one's own cultural identity is just as illogical as ignoring the customs and beliefs of the people in the other cultures with which we interact.[11]

The advancement of technology, particularly communication technology, has allowed an increasing number of nations to join the world marketplace, creating diverse and complex global environments that require organizations to engage in adaptive strategies to remain competitive.[12] We have a universal tendency to think that other people do things for the same reasons we do them.

When we understand our own culture, it helps to keep us from assuming the actions of people with different cultural backgrounds indicate the same meaning as when we act that way. As we become more aware of the assumptions and values on which our own behavior and thinking rest, we can begin to contrast these assumptions and values with those of others. Going through this process helps sensitize us to the immense shortcomings of stereotyping others according to cultural norms.

In seeking to understand oneself and how they are influenced by their national culture, the individual begins to develop a knowledge of CQ.[13] "Individuals who are culturally intelligent are able to see past the stereotypes that a superficial understanding of cultural values provides. Those values are only a first step, knowledge CQ, of developing CQ."[14] CQ includes having information about different cultures and what they value, but it begins with understanding the individual person.

Globalization is increasing diversity in our communities and escalating complexity of the social environments within which organizations operate. The increase of more nations engaging in the global marketplace is introducing different patterns of thinking, ways of trading, negotiation styles, and business practices. Therefore, leaders must have finely tuned awareness of global perspectives, the capacity

Changed Mind, Changed Heart

for recognizing cultural synergies, and the ability to engage in continuous learning.[15] Unlike many of the other approaches to cross-cultural competency, CQ factors in the varying ways different personalities respond to cross-cultural interactions.

Livermore named four subdomains that compose CQ—knowledge CQ, interpretive CQ, perseverance CQ, and behavioral CQ—all of which overlap in some way.[16] Understanding and using these four subgroups is important in working with followers from multicultural communities.

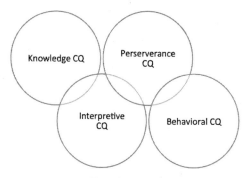

Figure 21. Four Subdomains of CQ.

Knowledge CQ

Knowledge CQ, also known as cognitive CQ, measures a person's understanding of cross-cultural issues and differences. This domain concentrates on understanding what culture is and how it shapes what we see.[17] A core component of knowledge CQ is understanding the notion of culture and how it interacts with what we all share as human beings versus what is unique to each of us as individuals.

Knowledge CQ is the domain most often emphasized when dealing with issues of cultural difference. This dimension of CQ is highly informational. The goal is not to master all the dos and don'ts of every culture we ever encounter, but to develop our overall cultural understanding and appreciation for how individual beliefs and practices are connected to their cultural background.

Cultural knowledge in and of itself is no guarantor of effectiveness, as cross-cultural training without the other aspects of CQ can actually hinder one's effectiveness. Leaders can increase their knowledge CQ by becoming more aware of culture's influence on the behaviors of self and others. One of the most important aspects of knowledge CQ is discerning when to look at something in light of culture, when to see something as common to all people, and when to see something as unique to one person.

Interpretive CQ

Interpretive CQ is the degree to which we are mindful and aware when we interact cross-culturally. This is the key process linking the understanding gained in knowledge CQ with the actual ability to apply it to how we behave.[18] It is almost impossible to separate interpretive CQ from knowledge CQ, which is why some researchers have kept them together under the umbrella of *cultural strategic thinking*.

Interpretive CQ begins with awareness of what lies beneath the external objects and behaviors in both the individual's environment and the environment of other people from other cultures. One has to intentionally become conscious of what lies beneath material things, appearance, reputation, social acceptance, and belonging.

We typically are not aware of the expectations and assumptions behind our own or others' behavior. Therefore, we have to settle for retrospective awareness discovered through intentional reflection, disciplining ourselves to see what we otherwise miss.[19] Awareness is important because most of the influences that shape our patterns of interpersonal interaction are unknown to us, and the patterns themselves are largely outside of our awareness.[20] The way we become more aware and more accurately interpret what we observe is largely tied to our level of cross-cultural understanding.

Interpretive CQ helps us get beyond slowing down to observe what is happening and moves us toward trying to accurately interpret the meaning behind what we observe. It gets us below the objects of culture to understand the values and assumptions of a culture. Interpretive CQ will teach us how to determine whether language issues, such as asking someone where he or she stays as opposed to where he or she lives, are one-time exceptions to the way we would

Perseverance CQ

Perseverance, or motivational, CQ is based on one's level of interest, drive, and motivation to adapt cross-culturally. Individualized emotions experienced within different cultural contexts are an essential consideration for understanding the dynamic nature of cross-cultural interactions.[21] Self-efficacy, the perception we have of our ability to reach a goal, is the central aspect of how we engage the world and the circumstances and people we encounter.

It is our confidence in our ability to accomplish a specific action that helps us coherently organize our skills, emotions, and frame of mind as we tackle a new challenge. It results in a proactive approach to life rather than a reactive one. There's a positive relationship between self-efficacy and CQ. "Without a strong sense of self-efficacy, a person will avoid challenges and give up easily when confronted with setbacks. The motivational aspect of cultural intelligence requires a personal sense of efficacy and desire for enactive mastery."[22] The self-efficacy needed for perseverance CQ draws on all four factors, though it fits most squarely in the motivational one.

Changed Mind, Changed Heart

Behavioral CQ

The final subdomain of CQ is behavioral CQ. This is the extent to which we appropriately change our verbal and nonverbal actions when we interact cross-culturally and the one factor of CQ by which we are most often judged.[23] The challenge of behavioral CQ is knowing when it is appropriate to change our behavior from how we would act in our own cultural context and when it is not appropriate. The goal of this subdomain is to be yourself while figuring out which behaviors need to change in order to lovingly express who you are as a leader.

The most effective way to manipulate you behavior is through the other three factors of CQ: knowledge CQ, interpretive CQ, and perseverance CQ. Behavioral CQ—primarily the outcome of our understanding, thinking, and motivation—is not truly a cultural adjustment but an adjustment to people's behavior. Behavior is the principal manifestation and most significant consequence of culture that we actually experience.[24]

"It is culture as encountered in behavior that we must learn to live with."[25] We have to adjust to behaviors of other people who annoy or confuse us. And we have to adjust our own behavior so that it does not needlessly annoy or confuse the other. There are two types of behaviors. Type 1 behaviors are those actions of people in the other cultures that annoy us, and the kinds of behavior to which we must learn to appropriately adapt or accept. Type 2 behaviors are the things we do that are offensive to others. Behavior is confusing, as the same action can have many different meanings. There are some basic behaviors we simply need to hone before interacting with people in certain contexts.

Coaching with Cultural Intelligence

Coaching to change the culture of an organization to align it more with the beliefs and values of the leadership can be challenging. But in servant-leadership coaching, there is an even larger challenge to not only encompass the organizational culture but the subcultures within as well. It is, however, not impossible as the main premise of the servant-leadership model to coach change in the organizational culture to support the community through acceptance of all cultures. This is possible by utilizing the tools of CQ in the coaching process.

Gary Collins outlined four core guidelines for coaching across cultural boundaries: self-awareness, cultural awareness, learning perspective, and servant mentality. In looking deeper into these four core guidelines, we understand that the first, self-awareness, refers to the coach being aware of his or her own assumptions, values, worldviews, and perspectives of how things should be done.[26] Coaches must take into consideration the cultural differences of others and that everything will not always be as it is where they are trained.

The second, cultural awareness, is that coaches should be sensitive to other cultures. In other words, put into practice the knowledge of CQ and show the concern of the other culture, adjusting to the difference that may be present. The third, learning perspective, refers to the cultural differences in learning. Not all adults learn the same way, which is in part due to their cultural beliefs. And the final, servant mentality, is in line with what this model is all about—remembering to be sensitive, humble, authentic, and respectful, open to new ideas, and being a servant first and foremost.[27]

Summary

Every person has been created a unique human being. We have similar qualities, but we have those that are unique to our culture, to our world. It is understandable that when faced with situations that involve a different culture, we may be challenged to adapt.

When wrestling with our cultural assumptions in tension with our own values, we will begin to see the aspects of our cultural perspective that should change, as well as ways we need to be agents of change among others. CQ is a two-way street. It is up to us to change our behavior to conform to others. At the same time, many of our cross-cultural encounters do not involve clear distinctions of guest and host. So we need to explore ways to make CQ something we encourage both in directions.[28] The richest cross-cultural relationships involve CQ flowing both ways.

Globalization is a reality in twenty-first-century organizations. Diversity is all around us, and growth of the multicultural organization is unavoidable. It is imperative that leaders function effectively in cross-cultural situations as well as in domestic situations. CQ, while not new, is newly recognized in organizations and throughout leadership research circles today. How it affects leader's communication effectiveness, strategic planning, decision-making, negotiation, conflict resolution, team building, and information sharing, while working with diverse cultural groups and in new global settings, will require more research.

However, it is necessary to incorporate CQ competencies in our strategic plans, making training available to our leadership teams if we desire to be a competitive player in the global scene. The twenty-first-century leader must become a lifelong learner, honing the skills of CQ in order to be competitive in this ever-changing diverse world. CQ is an essential skill to be taught and practiced in our twenty-first-century organizations around the globe.

Merging the principles of CQ and servant-leadership will bring change to our organizations. Through coaching initiatives, we will see these changes not only survive but thrive. People will see a new servant-leader emerge in the service industry; the word *service* will be put back into practice; and people will once again be the focal point of the organization.

11

Showing Genuine Concern to the Community

Preservation of one's own culture does not require contempt or disrespect for other cultures.

—Cesar Chavez

Being raised in the South during the early 1960s, I was in the midst of the Civil Rights Movement, living in a world where one race lived in one area and the other in another without comingling except to work where it was *permissible*. It was not until later in adulthood that I experienced different cultural values between races.

Here we are, nearly fifty years after the Civil Rights Movement ended, seeing issues with race rise up again with hate crimes and terrorist threats at the highest levels in history.[1] Why is it so many people have a problem getting along? The United States is more diverse now than in the past, the world is changing, borders are shrinking, and it is less expensive and more effortless to travel globally than it was in past years. Yet we still see instances of dispute within our communities based on equality and racial disparity. Why?

One of the reasons is our cultural awareness and our commitment to genuinely care for other people regardless of race, nationality, gender, or economic status. While it is easier than ever before to travel and communicate across borders, the world we live in is getting harsher toward each other.[2] I believe some of the reason for the shortage of cultural awareness is a lack of respect and understanding for people from different walks of life. So many times, we feel that others should fit into our mold, our life, and give up everything they know and love. We expect others to conform to us, but we do not tolerate conforming to others. Where is the middle of the road on the issues of cultural awareness and acceptance?

Not only do we have cultural issues between races and nationalities, but we have to take into consideration all the subcultures. There is an individual culture, race, nationality, organization, and family culture, just to name a few, that make a difference in how churches, service organizations, and nonprofit charitable organizations operate. Culture is the individual's, organization's, or group's "unwritten rules, values, norms, behaviors and other practices that collectively define how work gets done."[3]

Changed Mind, Changed Heart

Coaching an organization through cultural change is an important aspect of servant-leadership coaching. Therefore, the next step in the model is showing genuine concern to the community. This can be accomplished by understanding the culture of the community and changing the culture of the community through the coaching process.

Figure 22. Servant-Leadership Coaching Model, Stage 3, Phase 3.

Emotional Intelligence

People are more influenced by leaders' soft skills than their technical skills. Their interpersonal skills are what matter most—that ability to communicate, motivate, and show genuine concern for others. Soft skills are an important aspect of creating highly productive followers. When leaders lack these skills or actively cultivate their hard-edged opposite, followers will abandon the organization. A basic soft skill important to explore for leaders and coaches is that of emotional intelligence (EI)—the intersection of intelligence (i.e., the ability to learn, acquire knowledge, and solve problems) and emotion (i.e., the ability to help people cope, survive, and thrive in their environment). Emotions are necessary and critical for effective decision-making.[4]

One small act of kindness goes a long way to show followers you truly care about them and who they are as a person. EI helps leaders and coaches understand more about why we do what we do. Understanding emotions includes the knowledge of how they change, progress, and transition from one state to another.[5] Learning to manage emotions and coach others to manage their emotions allows a person to learn to extract data from them and use that data in decision-making and behaviors. These are important concepts for leaders of churches, charitable organizations, and service industries to become knowledgeable and skilled in when utilizing the servant-leadership coaching model. By modeling these behaviors, you turn around the way customers, followers, and observers are treated, and you demonstrate a genuine concern for their well-being, empowering them to be more.

Genuine Concern

To show concern for others, we must have the attitude of compassion, being sympathetic and tenderhearted toward the distress and adversity of others. Compassion demands action and works.

According to *The Enterprise—Utah's Business Journal*, a survey of one thousand doctors was taken concerning patient care and being sued. Doctors who spent at least sixteen minutes or more being sincerely interested in their patients, even if they made grave errors, were usually forgiven by their patients. This was due to people feeling their doctor cared them, which made them more understanding in light of the errors. However, for every minute under sixteen that doctors did not spend being sincerely interested in their patients, the chance of being sued was increased by 10 percent.[6]

Compassion is exemplified throughout the Bible, and those with biblical values often exhibit this trait. However, it is possible for everyone to exhibit love and compassion for others. Unfortunately, the word *compassion* is often associated with the word *sympathy*, implying something bad has happened to a person or group, therefore, we feel compassion for that person or group.[7] However, I contend that compassion can be felt for people or groups regardless of whether they have been through something, whether bad or good has affected them. We can and should show compassion to those in the world as a symbol of love and care for one another. This can be accomplished through proper communication, being kind, showing hospitality and discretion, and learning and acceptance of other cultures.

Communication

Human communication is becoming a thing of the past due to technological and economic achievements.[8] Through conversation, we can learn the background of others, find common interests, and discern others' needs. Empathy is one of the greatest ways we can show loving concern. By giving people time to both express their joys and concerns, we make that statement that we care.

Concern can be shown through communication with something as simple as taking a coffee break with employees. Identify with the needs of others by putting yourself in their shoes for just a moment. Listen and learn who they are, as the culture is the environment or context in which the act of communication takes place.[9] You might just find a gift that can catapult the organization to the next level, all by making someone feel special enough to be heard.

Show Kindness

Remember the Golden Rule? "Do unto others as you would have them do unto you" can be found in some form or fashion in many world religions, including Judaism, Christianity, Islam, Hinduism, Buddhism, and Confucianism.[10] The Golden Rule asks us to be considerate of others rather than indulging in self-centeredness.[11]

Little acts of kindness mean a lot in an ever-changing world. By giving others a little of your time as you help them out, they feel special. They feel a part of what is happening. Kindness is a gift that keeps on giving and is contagious. Leaders who show kindness to their followers receive respect in return. Many leaders demand respect, but true respect is developed through the kind deeds of the leader. I am often heard telling students respect begets respect.

Show Hospitality and Discretion

Extending hospitality is the essence of showing outgoing concern. It depends on the two virtues of generosity and finesse. Generosity is the commitment to offer the best you have with an open heart, and finesse is giving it that special touch that says "You are special."[12] Sharing your space builds bonds of attachment, showing others an environment of acceptance. Showing hospitality involves showing respect for others, providing for their needs, and treating them as equals. In different cultures or nationalities, the word *hospitality* has different meaning, but the root always conveys taking care of another person.

There are times when showing hospitality is simply allowing another to talk. When you show concern to others, they will almost always open up to you.[13] They may reveal some of their faults, weaknesses, or other personal hardships. The leader has an obligation to maintain privacy and confidence to the extent that no person is harmed by the information or actions of others. Love, concern, and compassion require we bear some of their difficulties and maintain their privacy. Being a servant-leader requires we show empathy during these conversations.

Learn and Accept Other Cultures

Genuine concern is a learned process.[14] As we learn about others and their needs, we begin to learn how to show genuine concern. Not only do leaders influence culture, they are influenced by it. Learning and accepting other cultures, those with different beliefs, can lead to some of our richest experiences of authentic spirituality of the heart. It comes through opening ourselves to share experiences of other cultures and spiritualties, of other members of human society.[15]

The world in which we live, work, and worship is changing every day. We are quickly becoming a borderless society in which change is inevitable. In becoming such a society, we must learn how to communicate with other cultures. While technology has given us affordable tools in which to communicate across the nations, communication is not simply learning a new language and sending e-mail, messaging, or video chatting. It is learning a new culture or a new way of doing business.[16] No longer is it only the responsibility of the high-level executive of an organization or the expatriate living amongst other culture to understand the difference in cultures.

It is up to each of us to learn and understand why people believe, act, and respond in ways that are different from us. The United States and other nations are becoming culturally diverse. There are new ways and ideas to be learned and utilized. In order to genuinely show care and compassion to people, we have to understand why they do the things they do; culture is the very heart of human society.[17] For that reason, I concentrate the remainder of this chapter on understanding cultural diversity.

Cultural Diversity

Cultural diversity is evident everywhere we go and is growing not only in the United States but around the globe. It embraces all manifestations of social habits of a community, the reactions of the individual as affected by the habits of the group, and the products of human activities are determined by these habits.[18] The effective cost of communication and travel has opened the door to cultural diversity, bringing in people who never dreamed they would ever step outside the borders of their own small community. Communication is a major issue in cultural diversity and one that must be addressed by leadership daily.

One of the key components to effective cross-cultural communication is knowledge. In the United States, we often feel our way is the right way, and we need to teach that way to other nations, other cultures. However, as our country grows in cultural diversity, it is important to understand other ideas and ways of doing things in order to properly communicate without strife or conflict.

It is essential that we understand the potential problems of cross-cultural communication, consciously attempting to overcome the hurdles associated with cultural diversity.

It is also important to assume that one's efforts will not always be successful and adjust behaviors accordingly, given that a different cultural context brings new communication challenges.[19] For example, when employees located in different locations or offices speak the same language, such as English (i.e., English speakers in the United States versus English speakers in the United Kingdom), there are cultural differences as well as dialect differences to consider, which will optimize communication between the two parties.

An effective communication strategy is one that addresses the cultural diversity by understanding the sender of the message and the receiver of the message are from different cultures and backgrounds. This complex communication makes it important to understand cultural factors that are involved.

Awareness of Individual Cultures

Learning the basics about culture and at least something about the language of communication in different countries is important. This is necessary even for the basic level of understanding required to engage in appropriate greetings, physical contact, and nonverbal communications, bonding with the people or simply understanding their personal preferences to doing business.

For instance, kissing a business associate is not considered an appropriate business practice in the United

States. However, in Paris, one peck on each cheek is an acceptable greeting. Another example would be the firm handshake that is widely accepted in the United States but is not recognized in all other cultures. From these examples, one can see that a person's behaviors and reactions are often culturally driven. While they may not match our own, they are culturally appropriate.

Cultural Factors

People communicate through a wide range of behavior that is unexamined and taken for granted. This process occurs outside of conscious awareness and in juxtaposition to words. What people do is frequently more important than what they say. Culture may be defined as the way of life of people of a certain region—the sum of their learned behavior patterns, attitudes, and material things. Culture controls behavior in deep and persisting ways, many of which are outside awareness and, therefore, beyond the individual's conscious control.

Edward T. Hall, anthropologist and one of the founders of intercultural communication study, has played a key role in describing how people's view of the world and behavior are largely determined by a complex grid of unconscious cultural patterns. Hall outlined a broad theory of culture and described how its rules control people's lives. Culture is a complex series of interrelated activities, with roots buried in the past in infraculture, behavior that preceded culture but later elaborated by humans into culture. Hall attempted to bring the behavior patterns of different ethnicities to awareness.

Hall found that, in some cultures, communication occurs predominantly through explicit statements in text and speech, which he categorized as low-context cultures. Low-context cultures communicate in direct, explicit, and informative ways. In low-context communication, information is more important than context; knowledge is public, external, and accessible; and communication is clear and short. Furthermore, in these cultures, human relationships begin easily and end quickly. For this reason, one's identity is rooted in one's accomplishment rather than that of family backgrounds. Communication is seen only as a way of exchanging information, ideas, and opinion.[20]

The other side of the coin is high-context communication, which is used in cultures where messages include other communicative cues such as body language and the use of silence. High-context communication involves implying a message through what is not uttered.[21] High-context means that "most information is either in the physical context or internalized in the person, while very little is in the coded, explicit, transmitted part of message."[22]

It has been said that Hall determined high-context cultures emphasized harmony, beauty, and oneness with nature, and confrontation and direct comparison are not favored.[23] People from high-context cultures are sensitive to specific surrounding circumstances and cherish interpersonal relationships. The people in these cultures believe knowledge is situational and relational. Relationships depend on trust, build up slowly, and last a long time.[24] The differences of high- and low-context cultures in Hall's model are summarized in Table 1.[25]

Table 1. *High-Context / Low-Context Culture Comparison.*

Factor	High-context Culture	Low-Context Culture
Overtness of messages	Many covert and implicit messages, with use of metaphor and reading between the lines	Many overt and explicit messages that are simple and clear
Locus of control and attribution for failure	Inner locus of control and personal acceptance for failure	Outer locus of control and blame of others for failure
Use of non-verbal communication	Much nonverbal communication	More focus on verbal communication than body language
Expression of reaction	Reserved, inward reactions	Visible, external, outward reaction

Cohesion and separation of groups	Strong distinction between in group and out-group. Strong sense of family	Flexible and open grouping patterns, changing as needed
People bonds	Strong people bonds with affiliation to family and community	Fragile bonds between people with little sense of loyalty
Level of commitment to relationships	High commitment to long-term relationships. Relationship more important than task	Low commitment to relationship. Task more important than relationships
Flexibility of time	Time is open and flexible. Process is more important than product	Time is highly organized. Product is more important than process

In his studies of cultural factors, Hall also distinguished between monochromic time (M-time) and polychromic time (P-time) to describe two contrasting ways of handling time in different cultures. Typically, M-time people do one thing at a time; P-time people multitask.[26]

In monochromic cultures, people tend to have a linear time pattern. North European and North American people are normally thought to be monochromic-time people. Conversely, polychromic people like to be involved in many things at once and are committed to people and personal relationships rather than to the job. They associate with the cyclic time pattern rather than with the linear time pattern. Most Asian countries are regarded polychromic. M-time people adhere rigorously to plans, while P-time people change plans often and easily. A summary of characteristics of monochromic and polychromic cultures is presented in Table 2.[27]

Table 2. *Monochromic/Polychromic Comparison.*

Factor	Monochromic action	Polychromic action
Actions	Do one thing at a time	Do many things at once
Focus	Concentrate on the job at hand	Are easily distracted
Attention to time	Think about when things must be achieved	Think about what will be achieved
Priority	Put the job first	Put relationships first
Respect for property	Seldom borrow or lend things	Borrow and lend things often and easily
Timeliness	Emphasize promptness	Base promptness relationship factors

Concern for Coaching

In chapter 10, we explored CQ and why it is important to the coaching process. In this chapter, we have explored cultural diversity and understanding of individual cultural issue in an effort to better understand how to show genuine concern to the community when crossing diverse cultures. Applying simple coaching technique can bring out the best in the organization, as well as in leaders and followers.

The culture of the organization exerts powerful influence on the performance. In this instance, coaching as a professional practice must move beyond being used only to develop the individual leader but be used as in-the-moment team coaching, group coaching, coach mentoring, coaching skills workshops, and other coaching-based approaches to bring about comprehensive change initiatives.[28]

With growth in the coaching industry, we see coaching-based initiatives are being leveraged to change company cultures in important and strategic ways.[29] The servant-leadership coaching model helps to strengthen the culture of the organization, in addition to guiding the leader and followers through the change initiatives to better understand the community cultures, member cultures, and organizational culture. A complete understanding of subcultures is necessary to make effective changes and operate in a servant-leader capacity.

Summary

Culture is communication, and communication is culture. When we look at the global world we live in, that statement comes to life. Culture is a way to communicate; at the same time, communication is a way of the cultures around the world. The world is becoming more diverse by the moment. Leadership today must grasp the new way of doing business and, in that new way, understand that other cultures have the *right way* also. A learning environment within our organizations is imperative if we are to communicate cross-culturally to be successful in our endeavors without offending anyone.

Humans seek to respond to the competitive pressures of power and limited resources in a rapidly globalizing and fragmented world through the development of cultures. The cultures we develop are not static entities but rather processes of "becoming based on hidden assumptions of political, gender and ideological power."[30]

To show genuine care, it is important to understand these cultural differences, not only in communication but in time management and behaviors as well. It is necessary for leaders to be on the learning end as well as the teaching end to help stop cultural illiteracy. By taking the time to understand individuals and their cultural differences, a leader shows that he or she not only cares but is ready to invest in the individuals, building confidence in people who, under other circumstances, may never grow to their fullest potential.

Understanding behaviors, why people do what they do, not only will stretch the mind and grow leaders in diversity but will also keep misunderstanding to a minimum, grow successful organizations, and help this world grow into what God intended it to be in the first place. Make genuine concern a focus in your business, emphasize it with your employees and volunteers, extend it to customers and members, and it will bring great success to your organization.[31]

12

Encouraging Change

You must be the change you wish to see in the world.

—Mahatma Gandhi

The moment of truth was finally here. All the secret planning and plotting was about to be revealed. There was a knock at the door, followed by the youth pastor walking in to submit his resignation. He had been praying for months about starting a church in the next town, and God had finally instructed him of the day and hour of which he was to make this move.

This was a very painful event for the senior pastor as the two men had been in ministry together for over fourteen years. They were best friends, and now he felt that his best friend, the man he thought would work hand in hand in ministry with him forever, had betrayed him. What made it worse was that his best friend had been plotting and planning behind his back for over nine months. The youth pastor had met with several members—leaders, no doubt—and convinced them to join him as his new staff in this new work. Thus, the church would not only lose the youth pastor but the assistant youth pastor, pianist, bass player, drama team leader, and associate pastor, as well as a dozen or so of the most faithful tithing members. This was a painful day that left the senior pastor, as well as his congregation, unsure as to the future of the church. The only certainty they had was knowing it was the beginning of major changes for the church. The next question, how would the congregation accept the changes that needed to be made?

This entire manuscript has been about change. The discussion has surrounded on the changes that need to take place and how coaching can lead us down the path of change. What has not yet been discussed is how change feels, how it is resisted, why it is resisted, and how we can help customers, members, and other stakeholders embrace the change. The final step to the servant-leadership coaching model is encouraging change. Change is difficult. But with the help of coaching, it can be encoaurged and embraced.

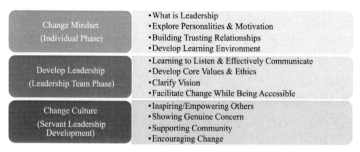

Figure 23. Servant-Leadership Coaching Model, Stage 4, Phase 4.

What to Do Next

Change is an ongoing and never-ending process in organizations, which can be frustrating for leaders because it is seldom an explainable, predictable, and controlled process that unfolds in unexpected ways.[1]

For leaders dealing with an organization going through change, it is very helpful to have a model of change in place. Models provide a perspective for sorting out these uncertainties.[2] Much of the literature concerning change has failed to recognize how difficult and painful it really can be. The programs and process for change they promote are often based on the assumption that everyone in an organization appreciates the need to change and is willing to work together to effect it, given the right tools.

While many changes in an organization's environment are often slow and subtle, it can be said that the change has been underway for some time before it is even noticed.

The story that opened this chapter is a good example: had there been talk of the youth pastor leaving and preparing, then most probably he would not have even given thought to the change. But the sudden uprooting and leaving gave rise to a crisis of sorts with the leaders and the followers. At this point, an understanding of the change process and what model of change would best fit with the organization is in order.[3]

The Resistance Movement

When sudden change occurs, the news is often a shock to those involved. More likely than not, this is the first of many changes to come, and each change is typically met with resistance—some from individuals and some from groups within the organization. Resistance is common. As with any change, you can expect stress, fear, hurt, and a feeling of rejection.[4]

In addition, leadership has to deal with followers resisting, grumbling, or complaining. Many resist because change requires them to move from the comfortable to something new and often uncomfortable.[5] They are uncomfortable because they have never done things the way they are now. They do not know what to expect or what will happen next. And many are afraid of failing.

In my experience, some people never resist change but adapt to it rather well due to being involved in an ever-changing organization. They tend to go with the flow or look for the next change around the corner. These people are extremely secure in their jobs and know what is going on at all times. A key to curbing the resistance movement is to communicate the change coming to the people. However, many organizations feel that change is not a necessary communication until it is ready to take place. This often causes rumors to begin and uneasy feelings among followers; nevertheless, it is the way organizations have operated for centuries. One thing we all must remember, change is necessary.

Keeping on Getting the Same Old Things

In the book *Leading Congregational Change*, the authors' first sentence of the preface sums up exactly why change is necessary: "If you keep doing what you've been doing, you'll keep getting what you've been getting."[6] In other words, in an organization, change is necessary. In order to understand how to change, the leaders must first understand the different types of change. Two common types are revolutionary and evolutionary.

The church mentioned at the beginning of this chapter underwent both types of change. They were thrust into a disruptive change, often referred to by experts as revolutionary change. After they survived those events, they found themselves in the midst of an evolutionary change. The youth pastor and other leaders leaving was a revolutionary change; it was an unexpected jolt to the church. It caused a revolution or rebellion in those who were not ready for the change.

However, through careful planning, this revolutionary change made a turn and over time became an evolutionary change, which lead to higher performance and improved the church. Although both types of change are usually needed in organizations, the revolutionary change is often painful, while the evolutionary change is slow to take place, almost going unnoticed at times.[7]

Within the constructs of evolutionary change are three distinct internal types of change: developmental, transitional, and transformational. Developmental change occurs when the organization is seeking to improve or correct a process, such as improving company billing procedures, updating payroll process, and so forth. These developmental changes are small incremental improvements in the way the organization conducts business.[8]

Transitional change is one in which the organization replaces an existing process or procedure with a new one. This type of change most often occurs within manufacturing systems where a manual production procedure may be replaced with an automated one. The change requires the organization to phase out the old method and implement the new procedure. Service organizations could go through this type of change when offering new products or services to increase revenue.[9]

Transformational change is a profound shift in the way an organization operates and typically involves developmental and transitional changes. A transformational change is implemented over time across all areas of the organization. Such changes result in transformation of the culture of the organization, such as restructuring the organization's business strategy.[10]

Planning for a Change

Making changes in organization can be an exciting prospect, one full of anticipation. Whether it is revolutionary or evolutionary, developmental, transitional, or transformational is for the leaders to decide. They can either force change, which "has the potential to create huge power outages or disconnections throughout an organization," or they can "identify and manage internal change processes designed to make organizations more competitive."[11] In other words, leaders can make a revolutionary change or practice planned change and make the transition evolutionary in nature.

Although there are times in leadership when revolutionary change is going to happen, it is best to focus on the evolutionary change. To do this, one must learn a skill we discussed earlier—strategic thinking. This is "a skill that will allow us to see and influence the future, today."[12] It is thinking and planning for the future by looking at the past trends and history of the organization. "Thinking strategically requires high-level cognitive skills, such as the ability to think conceptually, to absorb and make sense of multiple trends, and to condense all this information into a straightforward plan of action."[13]

Utilizing strategic thinking, leaders can plan for the future. They can make well-informed decisions as to what the future organization will be like and what the needs of the people will be, thereby determining what changes they will need to make as an organization. Then they can better plan for change, present the changes needed, and make adjustments along the way to the new and improved organization.

Steps to Change

Change does not just happen. The following steps should be followed before implementing change:

1. Gather information. Determine the subject of change. How is one seeking to change? What group or groups does the church want to reach? What are their needs? What is the current culture of the community? What will best attract these people? Determine your competitive advantage to the change and how best to implement the change to escalate the advantage.

2. Analyze the data collected. Compile the data and organize it in such a way as to give insight on how to

change in order to reach this new group of people. The data will paint the picture and show you clearly where to concentrate efforts for the best results.

3. Create an urgency for change before within the followers. Create excitement in the current organization about what is going to happen within the subcultures of the organization. Challenge the status quo and describe a compelling future—one of excitement for reaching and changing the community at large.

4. Restate the vision, mission, and goals. Restating the vision, mission, and goals will help followers and other leaders see that the changes are simply to keep the organization in line with the current purpose. Show those involved that you are not changing the vision, only expanding the parameters.

5. Implement the changes. Put the plan in motion. Start new programs—whatever data showed would work best to draw in the new crowd. Involve the current followers, employees, and volunteers alike to help implement the changes to make a better organization for all.

6. Reassess the plan. Set a date to evaluate what is working and what is not working and make adjustments as needed. Minor adjustments should be made along the way to keep the plan in working order.

7. Encourage the people. Encouragement goes a long way to relieving resistance. In order to lessen chaos and keep rumors from spreading, encourage people from the beginning.

Serving Through Encouraging

Encouragement is not a weakness of the leader but a strength. Encouragement makes a difference; it promotes a positive belief in others. We often take the value of encouragement for granted or sometimes miss it because it tends to be communicated privately rather than publically.

Rudolf Dreikurs said, "Humans need encouragement as much as plants need water. We constantly encourage or discourage those around us and thereby contribute materially to their greater or lesser ability to function."[14] Leaders who build people up are encouraging leaders, whose focus is on the resources that the follower's contribution can bring to the organization. To become a more encouraging leader, try the following four actions on your employees: identify positive potential in people and situations; communicate recognition, progress, and contributions; communicate with collaboration and cooperation; and be committed to coaching and feedback.

Identify Positive Potential in People and Situations

As servant-leaders, we must be able to not only see but embrace the potential in others. Everyone is unique. We must discover what that is. It requires effort and interest on the leader's part to learn about a team's potential. It begins with a servant mind-set, sound leadership development, and cultural coaching that teaches empowerment to all people. Encouraging leaders have a positive outlook toward life and recognize what others bring to the organization.

Communicate Recognition, Progress, and Contributions

Want to spruce up the morale in your organization? Then communicate how much you value other people's contributions. People want to know they are valued and that you appreciate what they do for the organization. They want to feel an internal connection with the organization and leadership. One way to enable them to feel this connection is to recognize their contributions. We must also continuously recognize progress and development toward the company's mission. By taking the time to communicate and recognize followers, we are communicating that we care and how much others mean to us. After all, organizations cannot exist without followers.

Communicate With Collaboration and Cooperation

Leadership is about how we share power with others. How do we share responsibility with others? It is with open, honest communication to create better collaboration and cooperation, understanding the power of *we* as opposed to *me*. We know we have succeeded at being an encouraging leader when people want to share ideas together and build relationships with one another.

Committed to Coaching and Feedback

Being a dedicated teacher or guide to our teams is part of building people up. We set aside valuable time to develop and mentor through our commitment to their success. By showing how much you desire them to flourish, you are adding value to members and teams. In addition to teaching and mentoring, you are open to feedback. You actually welcome that feedback to know how you are doing in their sight as a leader. This helps to build trust and encourage open feedback all the way around.

Summary

Change can be a painful process, struggling through the steps and losing relationships along the way. The church at the beginning of this chapter experienced the pain of revolution and the excitement of evolution. Strategic leadership—the process of providing the direction and inspiration necessary to create and sustain an organization—brought them together and was the key ingredient to this church becoming a healthy, successful church.

For so many years, pastors and church leaders have been thought of as uneducated, shallow people, but the truth is the new face of church leadership is one of cognitive thought processes that will carry the church to new levels. Those same processes can bring any leader of any organization to the same level. Teaching, encouraging, and empowering followers in the world today takes dedication, commitment, and a competitive spirit.

Revolutionary change can be very painful, but with the right tools and strategies, it does not have to be as painful. Knowing that revolutionary change is going to come from time to time, leaders can be better equipped to deal with the blows as they come and then coast through the evolutionary changes created through our carefully thought-out strategic plans. Education as how to plan for change and the types of change will help get through the valleys of change, so the church can experience the mountaintop newness that has been created.

All change is necessary in life. People cannot grow without change; how we one handled change is what will determine the success of the changes being made. Putting into practice the four behaviors of an encouraging leader can change the face of any organization, add productivity, and increase morale in followers and reshape the organization to reach new heights.

Change must happen, but it does not have to be devastating. The effect it has on people is up to the leader. The servant-leader is more concerned with seeing the follower through the change without scars and battle wounds than with coming out first and on top. The servant-leader is an encourager and leads the way to empower the follower to be the best that they can be at every turn and angle, thus making better organizations for today.

13

Servant-Leadership Coaching

The time has come to implement the servant-leadership coaching model. In the previous chapters, we talked about the elements needed in this coaching model as well as the elements needed to change an organization and the leadership to a servant-leadership organization. Now is time to implement the model and bring the best of both worlds together by coaching the organization and leader to be confident servant-leaders.

Being a servant-leader is more than just serving the people. Being a servant-leader requires spending time to build a relationship with the people, getting to know who they truly are, and learning what makes a difference in their world—showing people you care and are concerned about them. Being a servant-leader is desiring to change the world around as you teach others how to serve the needs of each other.

We explored each of the elements of servant-leadership coaching separately. To be successful, all elements must be combined into a solid model of leadership coaching and implemented as a whole. In other words, just because we change our mind-set to care more for people and take time to understand how their personality affects their motivation, developing who they are and why they do what they do does not make us a servant-leader. It is what we do with this information that transforms us into a leader who can transform lives and make a difference.

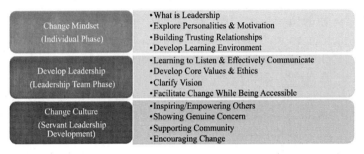

Figure 24. Servant-Leadership Coaching Model.

This model is designed with three phases: change the individual mind-set, develop the leader, and change the culture. Within each of these three phases are steps to achieve each phase. The job of the coach is to help guide the leader and/or followers through these steps.

Kathleen Patterson provided us with seven habits of the servant-leader. These seven habits—altruism, empowerment, humility, service, trust, and vision[1]—are taught within the constructs of the servant-leadership coaching model. As we explore the seven habits of the servant-leader and compare them with the twelve steps of the servant-leadership model, we can see how these habits are built into the model. Developing true servant-leaders through leadership coaching is the model's goal.

To summarize the model, let us review the steps. In changing the mind-set, we explore what is leadership. A solid foundation of the types of leadership such as transformational, transactional, and servant-leadership are discussed and reviewed with the client. From there, we move on to define and explain coaching and how coaching can help the leader to change and become more servant-oriented.

The next step is to grasp the difference in personalities, why and how our personality works together to build who we are, and how those personality differences affect our motivations for why we do what we do. In understanding the different personality types and motivations, the coach guides the leader through the process of how to utilize this information to build trusting relationships. Why are relationships built on trust so important to the leader and the organization? Servant-leadership, in the same way as coaching, is built on relationship and developing a trusting relationship with the follower. After all, how can one serve another's needs without trust, without knowing the other?

From that step, we develop the learning environment. The learning environment is significant in teaching not only current leaders to be servant-leaders but to promote leaders within the constructs of the organization. Learning is a lifetime process, and leaders should always be learning new trends, new products, new processes, and new developments.

From the individual aspect of the servant-leadership model, we move to the leadership development phase. In this phase, leaders are guided through learning to listen to their followers and communicate effectively with them. Servant-leaders are articulate communicators who understand how to talk to others and empower them to be all they can be. Coaches combine the skills of effective communication and listening with developing core values and ethics, clarifying vision and being accessible through the change process to help develop a healthy leader who can reach the people of the community and beyond.

Too many times, I have sat in church leadership meetings to hear how Jesus led but was never taught how I could lead like Jesus. Skill development was never an option in the meetings I attended. But through leadership coaching, these skills can be developed, and leaders can be taught how to communicate their values and vision to the people. They will learn how to give of themselves to the follower while still making time for family and personal development.

The final phase to the servant-leadership coaching model is changing the culture of the organization. The coach guides leaders by seeking an understanding of the subcultures present in their organization and developing an organizational culture to complement these subcultures. In doing so, leaders learn to show the compassion needed for the difference in the personal cultures the followers they work with.

When we understand differences, we can better work with the differences. People like to know they make a difference in this world. For this reason, empowerment is a key component within this model. With solid servant-leadership principles, leaders of the organization could empower those they lead, giving followers the ownership that makes a difference. Organizations will grow and thrive under new leadership as people begin to help one another and not simply complete a task for whatever is in it for them.

Servant-leaders carry many connotations. Some see servant-leaders as leaders of those who serve, while others see servant-leaders as weak leaders serving the whims of others. True servant-leaders, however, are those who through love and compassion bring out the best in those who follow them. In putting the servant-leadership coaching model into practice, leaders will learn not only about themselves but other people as well. They will learn about the human race and needs that God has instilled in each of us as humans.

The key to implementing this model is to choose a leadership coach wisely. Build that trusting relationship and begin to work through each phase one at a time. Put into practice what you learn and work closely with the coach. This process can be completed on an individual basis or with the organization as a whole. Coaches can use this model to teach leaders how to be more caring and compassionate and how to reach the needs of the people involved with the organization.

Change will create a falling domino effect, changing not only the people but the culture of the organization. As one organization changes and thrives, others will want to follow. The coach will utilize principles and ethical practices to see these changes take place. As the mind-set changes, the leader develops, the culture of the organization will change, and new heights will be reached.

Appendix A

The personality types developed by Myers and Briggs:

- Introversion–Sensing–Thinking–Judging (ISTJ). Individuals with this personality type are typically quiet, serious, dependable, practical, realistic, responsible, logical decision-makers, and take pleasure in being well-organized. They value traditions and loyalty.

- Introversion–Sensing–Feeling–Judging (ISFJ). Individuals with this personality type are typically quiet, friendly, responsible, conscientious, committed, accurate, loyal, and considerate, remembers specifics about people who are important to them, and are concerned with how others feel. They strive for orderly and harmonious work and home environments.

- Introversion–Intuition–Feeling–Judging (INFJ). Individuals with this personality type typically seek meaning and connection in ideas, relationships, and material possessions. They seek understanding as to motives of people, are insightful about others, conscientious and committed to their values, develop clear vision to serve the common good, organized and decisive in implementing vision.

- Introversion–Intuition–Thinking–Judging (INTJ). Individuals with this personality type typically are original thinkers with great drive for implementing ideas and achieving goals. They see patterns in external events, develop long-range explanatory perspectives, are committed, organized, skeptical and independent, and have high standards of competence and performance.

- Introversion–Sensing–Thinking–Perceiving (ISTP). Individuals with this personality type typically are tolerant, flexible, quiet observers who act quickly to find a workable solution when a problem arises. They analyze how things work while readily get through large amounts of data to isolate the core of practical problems. This individual is interested in cause and effect, organizes facts using logical principles, and value efficiency.

- Introversion–Sensing–Feeling–Perceiving (ISFP). Individuals with this personality type typically are quiet, friendly, sensitive, kind, enjoy the moment, like to have their own space and to work within their own time frame. They are loyal and committed to their values and to people who are important to them, dislike disagreements and conflicts, and do not force their opinions or values on others.

- Introversion–Intuition–Feeling–Perceiving (INFP). Individuals with this personality type typically are idealistic, loyal to their values and to people who are important to them but want an external life that is congruent with their values. They are curious, quick to see possibilities, can be catalysts for implementing ideas, seek to understand people and to help them fulfill their potential, are adaptable, flexible, and accepting unless a value is threatened.

- Introversion–Intuition–Thinking–Perceiving (INTP). Individuals with this personality type typically seek to develop logical explanations for everything that interests them, are theoretical and abstract, interested more in ideas than in social interaction, are quiet, contained, flexible, and adaptable. They have an unusual ability to focus in-depth to solve problems in their area of interest, are skeptical, sometimes critical, always analytical.

- Extroversion–Sensing–Thinking–Perceiving (ESTP). Individuals with this personality type typically are flexible, tolerant, take a pragmatic approach focused on immediate results, are bored by theories and conceptual explanations, focus on the here-and-now, and are spontaneous. They enjoy each moment that they can be active with others, material comforts and style, and they learn best through doing.

- Extroversion–Sensing–Feeling–Perceiving (ESFP). Individuals with this personality type are typically outgoing, friendly, accepting, exuberant lovers of life, people, and material comforts. They enjoy working with others, bring common sense and a realistic approach to their work, and make work fun. They are flexible and spontaneous, adapt readily to new people and environments and learn best by trying a new skill with other people.

- Extroversion–Intuition–Feeling–Perceiving (ENFP). Individuals with this personality type are typically warmly enthusiastic and imaginative, viewing life as full of possibilities. They make connections between events and information very quickly and confidently proceed based on the patterns they see. These individuals seek affirmation from others, readily give appreciation and support, are spontaneous and flexible, and often rely on their ability to improvise on their verbal fluency.

- Extroversion–Intuition–Thinking–Perceiving (ENTP). Individuals with this personality type are typically quick, ingenious, stimulating, alert, outspoken, and resourceful in solving new and challenging problems, adept at generating conceptual possibilities, and then analyzing them strategically. They are good at reading other people, bored by routine, will seldom do the same thing the same way, and are apt to turn to one new interest after another.

- Extroversion–Sensing–Thinking–Judging (ESTJ). Individuals with this personality type are typically practical, realistic, matter-of-fact, and decisive, organized, and focused on getting results in the most efficient way possible. They take care of routine details, have a clear set of logical standards, systematically follow, and are at times forceful in implementing their plans.

- Extroversion–Sensing–Feeling–Judging (ESFJ). Individuals with this personality type are typically warmhearted, conscientious, cooperative, and loyal. They like to work with others to complete tasks accurately and on time, follow through even in small matters, notice what others need in their day-by-day lives and try to provide it. They want to be appreciated for who they are and for what they contribute.

- Extroversion–Intuition–Feeling–Judging (ENFJ). Individuals with this personality type are typically warm, empathetic, responsive, responsible, loyal, responsive to praise and criticism, and sociable. They are highly attuned to the emotions, needs, and motivations of others. They find potential in everyone, want to help others fulfill their potential, may act as catalysts for individual and group growth, facilitate others in a group, and provide inspiring leadership.

- Extroversion–Intuition–Thinking–Judging (ENTJ). Individuals with this personality type are typically frank, decisive, assume leadership readily. They see illogical and inefficient procedures and policies, develop and implement comprehensive systems to solve organizational problems, enjoy long-term planning and goal setting. These individuals are well-informed, well-read, enjoy expanding their knowledge and passing it on to others, and are forceful in presenting their ideas.

Notes

1: Foundations of Servant Leadership Coaching

1. Gottfredson, M., & Markey, R. (2014). Focus on the customer. *Insights*. Retrieved from http://www.bain.com/publications/articles/focus-on-the-customer.aspx

2. Wren, D. (2005). *The history of Management Thought*. Oklahoma City, OK: John Wiley & Sons.

3. Winston, B. E., and Patterson, K. 2006. "An Integrative Definition of Leadership." *International Journal of Leadership Studies* 1(2), 6–66.

4. Parolini, J., Patterson, K., and Winston, B. 2009. "Distinguishing Between Transformational Leadership and Servant Leadership." *Leadership & Organization Development Journal* 30(3), 274–91.

5. Schneider, S. K., and George, W. M. (2009). "Servant Leadership Versus Transformational Leadership in Voluntary Service Organizations." *Leadership & Organization Development Journal* 32(1), 60–77.

6. Carey, W., Philippon, D., and Cummings, G. (2011, March). "Coaching Models for Leadership Development: An Integrative Review." *Journal of Leadership Studies* 5(1), 51–69.

7. Stoltzfus, T. (2005). *Leadership Coaching: The Disciplines, Skills and Heart of a Christian Coach.* Virginia Beach, VA: Author.

8. Keddy, J., and Johnson, C. (2011). *Managing Coaching at Work: Developing, Evaluating and Sustaining Coaching in Organizations.* London, UK: Kogan Page Limited, p. 5.

9. Keddy & Johnson, 2011, p. 5.

10. Haynor, P. (1994). "The Coaching, Precepting, and Mentoring Roles of the Leader Within an Organizational Setting." *Holistic Nurse Practitioner,* 9(1), 31–40. Joo, B. (2005). "Executive Coaching: A Conceptual Framework from an Integrative Review of Practice and Research." *Human Resource Development Review,* 4(4), 462–488. Milner, T., and Bossers, A. (2004). "Evaluation of the Mentor-Mentee Relationship in an Occupational Therapy

Programme." *Occupational Therapy International*, 11(2), 96–111.

11. Carey et al., 2011, p. 52.
12. Nielsen, A., and Norreklit, H. (2009). "A Discourse Analysis of the Disciplinary Power of Management Coaching. *Society and Business Review*, 4(3), 202–214.
13. Ibid, p. 207.
14. Whitmore, J. (1992). *Coaching for Performance*. London, UK: Nicholas Brealey.
15. McNally, K., and Lukens, R. (2006). "Leadership Development: An External-Internal Coaching Process." *Journal of Nursing Administration*, 36(3), 155–161.
16. Blattner, J., and Bacigalupo, A. (2007). "Using Emotional Intelligence to Develop Executive Leadership and Team and Organizational Development." *Consulting Psychology Journal: Practice and Research*, 59(3), 209–219.
17. Parker, P., Hall, D., and Kram, K. (2008). "Peer Coaching: A Relational Process for Accelerating Career Learning." *Academy of Management Learning & Education*, 7(4), 487–503.
18. Saporito, T. (1996). "Business-linked Executive Development: Coaching Senior Executives."

Consulting Psychology Journal: Practice and Research, 48(2), 96–103.

19. Sherman, S., and Freas, A. (2004, November). "The Wild West of Executive Coaching." *Harvard Business Review,* 82–90.

20. Kampa-Kokesch, S., and Anderson, M. (2001). "Executive Coaching: A Comprehensive Review of the Literature." *Consulting Psychology Journal: Practice and Research,* 53, 205–228.

21. Bennet, J., and Bush, M. (2009). "Coaching in Organizations." *OD Practitioner,* 41(1), 2–7.

22. Lingenfelter, S. G., and Mayers, M. K. (2003). *Ministering Cross-Culturally: An Incarnational Model for Personal Relationships.* Grand Rapids, MI: Baker Publishing Group.

23. Livermore, D. A. (2009). *Cultural Intelligence: Improving Your CQ to Engage Our Multicultural World.* Grand Rapids, MI: Baker Publishing Group.

24. Lingenfelter and Mayers, 2003.

25. Niebuhr, H. R. (1951). *Christ and Culture.* New York, NY: Harper & Row.

26. Kluckhohn, C., and Kroeber, A. L. (Eds.). (1952). *Culture.* New York, NY: Random House.

27. Becker, H. S. (1982). *Artworld.* Berkeley: University of California Press.

28. Hofstede, G. (1997). *Cultures and Organizations: Software of the Mind.* New York, NY: McGraw Hill.
29. Schein, E. (2004). *Organizational Culture and Leadership* (3rd ed.). San Francisco, CA: Jossey-Bass.
30. Hall, E. (1969). *The Hidden Dimension.* New York, NY: Anchor Books.

2: Exploring Personalities and Motivation

1. Maslow, A. H. (1970). *Motivation and Personality* (2nd ed.). New York, NY: Harper and Row.
2. Funder, D. C. (1997). *The Personality Puzzle.* New York, NY: Norton.
3. Moody, R. (1988). "Personality Preferences and Foreign Language Learning." *Modern Language Journal,* 72, 389–401.
4. The Myers and Briggs Foundation. (2015). *MBTI Basics.* Retrieved from http://www.myersbriggs.org/my-mbti-personality-type/mbti-basics/
5. Hirsh, S.K., and Kummerow, J.M. (1990). *Introduction to Type in Organizations* (2nd ed.). Mountain View, CA: Consulting Psychologists Press.
6. The Myers and Briggs Foundation. (2015). *MBTI Types.* Retrieved from http://www.myersbriggs.

org/my-mbti-personality-type/mbti-basics/the-16-mbti-types.htm

7. Ibid.

8. Zhang, W., Su, D., and Liu, M. (2013). "Personality Traits, Motivation and Foreign Language Attainment." *Journal of Language Teaching and Research*, 4(1), 58–66.

9. Winston, B. E. (2006). *Leadership Style as an Outcome of Motive: A Contingency "State" Rather Than "Trait" Concept*. Unpublished manuscript, Regent University, Virginia Beach, VA, pp. 1-9.

10. Levin-Gutierrez, M. (2015). "Motivation: Kept Alive Through Unschooling." *Journal of Unschooling and Alternative Learning*, 9(17), 31–41.

11. Zhang et al., 2013, p. 59.

12. Wren, D. A., and Bedeian, A. G. (2010). *The Evolution of Management Thought* (formerly *The history of management thought*). New York, NY: John Wiley & Sons, pp. 339–342.

13. Winston, 2006, p. 1.

14. Wren and Bedeian, 2010, p. 340.

15. Spreier, S. W., Fontaine, M. H., and Malloy, R. L. (2006, June). "Leadership Run Amok: The Destructive Potential of Overachievers." *Harvard Business Review*, 72–82.

16. Pink, D. (2009). *Drive: The Surprising Truth About What Motivates Us.* New York, NY: Riverhead Books.

17. McClelland, D. C. (1961). *The Achieving Society.* Princeton, NJ: Van Nostrand.

18. Spreier et al., 2006.

19. Winston, 2006, p. 2.

20. Ibid, p. 2.

21. Ibid, p. 8.

22. Al-Mailam, F. F. (2004). "Transactional Versus Transformational Style of Leadership-Employee Perception of Leadership Efficacy in Public and Private Hospital in Kuwait." *Quality Management in Health Care,* 13(4), 278–284.

23. House, R. J. (1977). A 19theory of charismatic leadership. In J. G. Hunt and L. L. Larson (Eds.), *Leadership: The cutting edge* (pp. 189). Carbondale: Southern Illinois University Press.

24. Winston, 2006, p. 8.

25. Ibid, p. 4.

26. Barbuto, J. E., Jr. (2005). "Motivation and Transactional, Charismatic, and Transformational Leadership: A Test of Antecedents." *Journal of Leadership and Organizational Studies,* 11(4), 26–40.

27. Bass, B. M. (1997). "Does the Transactional–Transformational Leadership Paradigm Transcend Organizational and National Boundaries?" *American Psychologist*, 52(2), 130–139.

28. Northouse, P. (2006). *Leadership: Theory and Practice* (4th ed.). Thousand Oaks, CA: Sage.

29. Winston, 2006, p. 5.

30. Northouse, 2006.

31. Winston, 2006, p. 6.

32. Greenleaf, R. K. (1970). *The Servant as Leader*. Newton Centre, MA: Robert K. Greenleaf Center.

33. Northouse, 2006.

34. Winston, 2006, p. 7.

35. Ibid, p. 8.

36. Burns, J. M. (1978). *Leadership*. New York, NY: Harper & Row.

37. Northouse, 2006.

38. Winston, 2006, p. 8.

39. Ibid, p. 8.

40. Ibid, p. 8.

41. Pryor, R. (2008). "Is Your Coaching Taking People In the Right Direction?" *People Management*, 14(3), 44.

42. Dow, L. (2010). "What Drives Those in the Driver's Seat?" *Directors and Boards*, 34(3), 58–61.

43. Nguni, S., Sleegers, P., and Denessen, E. (2006). "Transformational and Transactional Leadership Effects on Teachers' Job Satisfaction, Organizational Commitment and Organizational Citizenship Behavior in Primary Schools: The Tanzanian Case." *School Effectiveness and School Improvement*, 17(2), 145–177.

3: Building the Trusting Relationship

1. International Coach Federation. (n.d.). *Core Competencies*. Retrieved from http://coachfederation.org/credential/landing.cfm?ItemNumber=2206&navItemNumber=576

2. International Association of Coaching. (2014). *The IAC Coaching Masteries*. Retrieved from http://www.certifiedcoach.org/index.php/get_certified/the_iac_coaching_masteries_overview/

3. Relationship. (2015). In *Dictionary.com*. Retrieved from http://dictionary.reference.com/browse/relationship

4. Sobel, A., and Panas, J. (2014). *Power Relationships: Irrefutable Laws for Building Extraordinary Relationships*. Hoboken, NJ: John Wiley & Sons.

5. *Trust, the Foundation of Relationships.* (2013). Retrieved from http://www.leadership-with-you.com/trust.html

6. Kouzes, J. M., and Posner, B. Z. (2010). *The Truth About Leadership: The No-fads, Heart-of-the-Matter Facts You Need to Know.* San Francisco, CA: Josey-Bass.

7. His-An, S. Chiang, Y-H., and Chen, T. (2012). "Transformational Leadership, Trusting Climate, and Knowledge-Exhange Behaviors in Taiwan." *International Journal of Human Resource Management*, 23(6), 1057–1073.

8. Harper, S. (2012). "The Leader Coach: A Model of Multi-style Leadership." *Journal of Practical Consulting*, 4(1), 22–31.

9. Sobel and Panas, 2014, p. 67.

10. Thomas, G., Martin, R., Epitropaki, O., Guillaume, Y., and Lee, A. (2013). "Social Cognition in Leader-Follower Relationships: Applying Insights from Relationship Science to Understanding Relationship-Based Approaches to Leadership." *Journal of Organizational Behavior,* 34, S63–S81.

11. Clark, M. S., and Reis, H. T. (1988). "Interpersonal Processes in Close Relationships." *Annual Review of Psychology*, 39, 609–672.

12. Thomas et al., 2013, p. S64.
13. Northhouse, 2006, p. 12.
14. Goh, J. (2009). "Parallel Leadership in an "Unparallel" World: Cultural Constraints on the Transferability of Western Educational Leadership Theories Across Cultures." *International Journal of Leadership in Education,* 12(4), pp. 319–345, p. 324.
15. Clark, K. E., and Clark, M. B. (1999). "Chapter 13: Leadership and Cultural Differences." *Choosing to Lead.* Retrieved from http://0-ehis.ebscohost.com.library.regent.edu/ehost
16. O'Reilly, C.A., III, Chatman, J., and Caldwell, D. F. (1991). "People and Organizational Culture: A Profile Comparison Approach to Assessing Person-Organization Fit." *Academy of Management Journal,* 34(3), 487.
17. Goh, 2009, p. 324.
18. G. Thomas et al., 2013, p. S67.
19. Northhouse, 2006, p. 29.
20. ICF, n.d.
21. Sobel and Panas, 2014, p. 107.
22. Sills, C. (2003, February). "Towards the Coaching Relationship." *Masterclass, Training Magazine.* Retrieved from http://www.ashridge.org.uk

23. Collins, G. (2009). *Christian Coaching: Helping Others Turn Potential Into Reality.* Colorado Springs, CO: NavPress.

24. Sobel and Panas, 2014, p. 61.

4: Developing a Learning Environment

1. Lines, R., Saenz, J., and Aramburu, N. (2011). "Organizational Learning as a By-product of Justification For Change." *Journal of Change Management,* 11(2), 163–1845.

2. Senge, P. M. (2006). *The Fifth Discipline: The Art & Practice of the Learning Organization.* New York, NY: Doubleday.

3. Lines et al., 2011.

4. Kim, J., Kim, J., and Miner, A. (2009). "Organizational Learning From Extreme Performance Experience: The Impact of Success and Recovery Experience." *Organization Science,* 20(6), 958–978.

5. March, J. G., and Olsen, J. P. (1975). "The Uncertainty of the Past: Organizational Learning Under Uncertainty." *European Journal of Political Research, 3,* 147–171.

6. Argyris, C., and Schon, D. A. (1978). *Organizational Learning a Theory of Action Perspective.* Reading, MA: Addison-Wesley.

7. Spitzeck, H. (2009). "What, if Anything, Do Corporations Learn from NGO Critique?" *Journal of Business Ethics*, 88(1), 157–173.

8. Argyris, C. (1977, September). "Double-loop Learning in Organizations." *Harvard Business Review*, 115–124. Retrieved from https://hbr.org/1977/09/double-loop-learning-in-organizations/ar/1

9. Holmqvist, M. (2004). "Experiential Learning Processes of Exploitation and Exploration Within and Between Organizations: An Empirical Study of Product Development." *Organization Science*, 15(1), 70–81.

10. Lines et al., 2011.

11. Dutton, J. E., Ashford, S. J., O'Neill, R. M., and Lawrence, K. A. (2001). "Moves That Matter: Issue-selling and Organizational Change." *Academy of Management Journal*, 44(4), 716–736.

12. Neale, S., Spencer-Arnell, L., and Wilson, L. (2009). *Emotional Intelligence Coaching: Improving Performance for Leaders, Coaches and the Individual*. Philadelphia, PA: Kogan Page Ltd.

13. Audia, P. G., Locke, E. A., and Smith, K. G. (2000). "The Paradox of Success: An Archival and a Laboratory Study of Strategic Persistence Following Radical Environmental Change." *Academy Management Journal*, 43(5), 837–853.

14. Spitzeck, 2009, pp. 157–173.
15. Lines et al., 2011, p. 164.
16. Kolb, D. A. (1984). *Experiential Learning: Experience as the Source of Learning and Development.* Englewood Cliffs, NJ: Prentice-Hall.
17. Cyert, R., and March, J. G. (1992). *A Behavioral Theory of the Firm* (2nd ed.). Oxford, UK: Blackwell.
18. ICF, n.d.
19. IAC, 2014.

5: Learning to Listen and Communicate Effectively

1. Al-Omari, A., and Al-Mahasneh, R. (2011). "Listening Skills Among Undergraduate Students at the Hashemite University." *International Journal of Applied Educational Studies*, 10(2), 47–58.
2. ICF, n.d.
3. Al-Omari and Al-Mahasneh, 2011, p. 47.
4. Ibid, p. 48.
5. Watson, K. W., and Barker, L. L. (1995). *Listening Styles Profile.* Toronto, Ontario: Pfeiffer and Company.
6. Al-Omari and Al-Mahasneh, 2011, p. 49.

7. Ibid, p. 49.
8. Ibid, p. 49.
9. Al-Omari and Al-Mahasneh, 2011, p. 49.
10. Ripley, R., and Watson, K. (2014). "We're Learning—Are You Listening?" *Chief Learning Officer*, 13(5), 34–37.
11. Collins, 2009, p. 101.
12. Ibid, p. 101.
13. Behera, A. K. (2010). "Listening, An Art?" *Language in India, 10*, 12.
14. Collins, 2009, p. 102.
15. Behera, 2010.
16. Welch, S. A., and Mickelson, W. T. (2013). "A Listening Competence Comparison of Working Professionals." *International Journal of Listening, 27*(2), 85–99.
17. Schilling, D. (2012). "10 Steps to Effective Listening." *Forbes*. Retrieved from http://www.forbes.com/sites/womensmedia/2012/11/09/10-steps-to-effective-listening/
18. Collins, 2009, p. 100.
19. Gudykunst, W., and Kim, Y. (2002). *Communicating With Strangers: An Approach to Intercultural*

Communication (4th ed.). Boston, MA: McGraw-Hill, p. 430.

20. Communication. (2015). In *Merriam-Webster Dictionary Online*. Retrieved from http://www.merriam-webster.com/dictionary/communication

21. Rosen, R., Digh, P., Singer, M., and Philips, C. (2000). *Global Literacies: Lessons on Business Leadership and National Cultures*. New York, NY: Simon and Schuster, p. 98.

22. Ibid, p. 99.

23. Livermore, 2009, p. 213.

24. Collins, 2009, p. 100.

25. Ibid, p. 100.

6: Developing Ethical Leadership with Core Values

1. Hirchler, B. (2013). "GlaxoSmithKline to Stop Paying Doctors to Promote Drugs." *The Huffington Post*. Retrieved from http://www.huffingtonpost.com/2013/12/17/glaxosmithkline-pay-doctors_n_4457286.html

2. Ingram, D., and Krasny, R. (2013). "Johnson & Johnson to Pay $2.2 Billion to End U.S. Drug Probes." *Reuters*. Retrieved from http://

www.reuters.com/article/2013/11/04/us-jnj-settlement-idUSBRE9A30MM20131104

3. BBC News UK. (2012). *Phone Hacking: Five Files on Journalists Handed to CPS*. Retrieved from http://www.bbc.com/news/uk-18401624

4. Anderson, N. (2014). "Sex Offense Statistics Show U.S. College Reports are Rising." *The Washington Post*. Retrieved from http://www.washingtonpost.com/local/education/sex-offense-statistics-show-us-college-reports-are-rising/2014/07/01/982ecf32-0137-11e4-b8ff-89afd3fad6bd_story.html

5. Piotrowski, C., and Guyette, R. W., Jr. (2010). "Toyota Recall Crisis: Public Attitude on Leadership and Ethics." *Organizational Development Journal*, 28(2), 89–94.

6. Minkes, A. L., Small, M. W., and Chatterjee, S. R. (1999). "Leadership and Business Ethics: Does IT Matter? Implications for Management." *Journal of Business Ethics*, 20(4), 327–335.

7. Banerjea, P. K. (2010). "Wholesome Ethical Leadership." *The IUP Journal of Corporate Governance*, 4(1), 7–14.

8. McCann, J., and Holt, R. (2008). "Ethical Leadership and Organizations: An Analysis of Leadership in the Manufacturing Industry Based on the Perceived

Leadership Integrity Scale." *Journal of Business Ethics*, 87, 211–220.

9. Ciulla, J. B. (Ed.). (2004). *Ethics: The Heart of Leadership* (2nd ed.). Westport, CT: Praeger.

10. Ibid, p. 24.

11. Bouden, R. (2001). *The Origin of Values: Sociology and Philosophy of Beliefs*. New Brunswick, NJ: Transaction.

12. Joas, H. (2000). *The Genesis of Values*. Chicago, IL: University of Chicago.

13. Ibid, p. 132.

14. Ibid, p. 133.

15. Fayolle, A., Basso, O., and Legrain, T. (2008). "Corporate Culture and Values: Genesis and Sources of L'Oréal's Entrepreneurial Orientation." *Journal of Small Business & Entrepreneurship*, 21(2), 215-229.

16. Ibid, p. 217.

17. Cameron, K. S., and Quinn, R. E. (2006). *Diagnosing and Changing Organizational Culture: Based on the Competing Values Framework* (3rd ed.). San Francisco, CA: Jossey-Bass.

18. Green, D. D. (2008). "Value Transformation in 21st Century Organizations." *Journal of Organizational Culture, Communications & Conflict*, 12(2), 95–102.

19. Kidder, R. M. (2001). "Ethics is Not Optional." *Association Management*, 53(13), 30–32.

20. Ibid.

21. Waller, J. (2010). "Creating Ethical Business Standards Adopt a Modern Ethics Policy and Make it Public." *Alaska Business Monthly*, 26(4), 100–101.

22. Beekun, R. I., Westerman, J., and Barghouti, J. (2005). "Utility of Ethical Frameworks in Determining Behavioral Intention: A Comparison of the U.S. and Russia." *Journal of Business Ethics*, 61(3), 235–247.

23. Schein, E. H. (1997). *Organizational Culture and Leadership.* San Francisco, CA: Jossey-Bass.

24. Sauser, W. I., Jr. (2013). "Empowering Leaders to Craft Organizational Cultures of Character: Conceptual Framework and Examples." *Journal of Leadership, Accountability and Ethics,* 10(1), 14–29.

7: Clarifying the Vision in Terms of Strategic Planning

1. Walesh, S. G. (2008). "Vision: Pie-in-the-Sky or Organizational Priority?" *Leadership & Management in Engineering,* 8(1), 45–46.

2. Snyder, N. H., and Graves, M. (1994). "Leadership and Vision." *Business Horizons*, 37(1), 1–7.
3. Collins, 2009, p. 171.
4. Snyder and Graves, 1994, p. 2.
5. Collins, 2009, p. 173.
6. O'Connell, D., Hickerson, K., and Pillutla, A. (2011). "Organizational Visioning: An Integrative Review." *Group & Organization Management*, 36(1), 103–125.
7. Ibid, p. 110.
8. Ibid, p. 111.
9. O'Brien, F., and Meadows, M. (2000). "Corporate Visioning: A Survey of UK Practice." *Journal of the Operational Research Society*, 51, 36–44.
10. O'Connell et al., 2011, p. 111.
11. Ibid, p. 111.
12. Ibid, p. 112.
13. Bunker, B. B., and Alban, B. T. (2006). *The Handbook of Large Group Methods: Creating Systemic Change in Organizations and Communities.* San Francisco, CA: Jossey-Bass.
14. Hill, C. W. L., and Jones, G. R. (2010). *Strategic Management: An Integrated Approach* (9th ed.). Mason, OH: South-Western Cengage Learning.

15. Sanders, T. I. (1998). *Strategic Thinking and the New Science*. New York, NY: The Free Press, p. 135.

16. Ibid, p. 10.

17. Bass, B. M., and Steidlmeier, P. (1999). "Ethics, Character, and Authentic Transformational Leadership Behavior." *Leadership Quarterly*, 10(2), 181–217.

18. Daft, R. L. (2005). *The Leadership Experience*. Mason, OH: South-Western, p. 153.

19. Sanders, 1998, p. 51.

20. Ibid, p. 52.

21. Hamidizadeh, M. R., and Shahri, M. H. (2007). "Designing a Model for Identifying, Assessing and Determining Strategic Capabilities: A Study in Iran." *Khodro, Quarterly Journal of Iran's Management Sciences*, 1(4), 1–28.

22. Daft, 2005, p. 528.

23. Johnson, C. E. (2005). *Meeting the Ethical Challenges of Leadership* (2nd ed.). Thousand Oaks, CA: Sage, p. 5.

24. Collins, 2009, p. 171.

25. Chinsky, D. (2007). "Executive Coaching." *Healthcare Executive*, 22(1), 50–53.

26. Collins, 2009, p. 171.

27. Ibid, p. 171.
28. Bradford, R., Duncan, J. P., and Tarcy, B. (2000). *Simplified Strategic Planning*. Worchester, MA: Chandler House Press, p. 159.

8: Facilitating Change While Being Accessible

1. Bala, K. (2014). "Social Media and Changing Communication Patterns." *Global Media Journal–Indian Edition*, 5(1), 1–7.
2. Ibid, p. 1.
3. ICF, n.d.
4. Kouzes and Posner, 2010.
5. Niederkohr, T. (2007). "Becoming a User-Friendly Leader." *Aftermarket Business*, *117*(8), 6. Retrieved from http://0-eds.b.ebscohost.com.library.regent.edu/ehost/pdfviewer/pdfviewer?vid=8&sid=a527f81b-b1be-4e4c-a4ab-5e7205b9a597%40sessionmgr113&hid=111
6. Feuer, M. (2011). "An Exaggerated Sense of Your Own Importance Can Stifle New Ideas." *Smart Business Cleveland*, 22(9), 90.
7. Yukl, G. A. (1981). *Leadership in Organizations*. Englewood Cliffs, NJ: Prentice-Hall.

8. Hanson, L. (2002). "What Boards Can do About America's Corporate Leadership Crisis." *NACD Directorship*, 28(4), 13.

9. Kuhnert, K. W., and Lewis, P. (1987). "Transactional and Transformational Leadership: A Constructive/Developmental Analysis." *Academy of Management Review*, 12(4), 648–657.

10. Burns, 1978.

11. Ibid., p. 4

12. Jones, H., & Lioba, I. (2004). "The Servant Leader." *Nursing Management*, 11(3), 20-24.

13. Finley, S. (2012). "Servant Leadership: A Literature Review." *Review of Management Innovation & Creativity*, 5(14), 135–144.

14. Ibid, p. 137.

15. Spears, L. (1996). *Insights on Leadership*. New York, NY: John Wiley & Sons.

16. McKibben, S. (2013). "Beyond the Open-Door Policy." *Education Update*, 55(9), 1–3.

17. Ibid, p. 3.

18. Ibid, p. 3.

19. Ibid, p. 3.

20. Hanson, 2002, p. 13.

21. Collins, 2009, p. 51.
22. McKibben, 2013, p. 3.

9: Inspiring Others Through Empowerment

1. Admin. (2014). "Carl's Garden." *Empowering Stories: Life is Short—Enjoy the Journey.* Retrieved from http://empoweringstories.com/inspire/carls-garden/
2. Rubio-Sanchez, A., Bosco, S. M., and Melchar, D. E. (2013). "Servant Leadership and World Values." *Global Studies Journal*, 5(3), 19–33
3. Ibid.
4. Russell, R. F., and Stone, A. G. (2002). "A Review of Servant Leadership Attributes: Developing a Practical Model." *Leadership & Organization Development Journal*, 23(3/4), 145–158.
5. Liden, R. C., Wayne, S. J., Zhao, H., and Henderson, D. (2008). "Servant Leadership: Development of a Multidimensional Measure and Multi-Level Assessment." *The Leadership Quarterly*, 19, 161–177.
6. Sauser, 2013, p. 15.
7. Orgambidez-Ramos, A., and Borrego-Ales, Y. (2014). "Empowering Employees: Structural

Empowerment as Antecedent of Job Satisfaction in University Settings." *Psychological Thought*, 7(1), 28–36.

8. Al-Shalabi, N. (2011). "Empowering Learners: Teaching American Literature By Shifting the Focus From the Instruction Paradigm to the Learning Paradigm." *International Forum of Teaching and Studies*, 7(2), 70–75.

9. Greenleaf, R. (1998). *The Power of Servant Leadership*. San Francisco, CA: Berrett-Koehler.

10. Ibid, p. 48.

11. Collins, 2009, p. 215.

12. Kouzes & Posner, 2010, p. 56.

13. Sauser, 2013, p. 15.

14. Melrose, K. (1996). "Putting Servant Leadership Into Practice." In L. Spears, *Insights on leadership* (pp. 284–287). New York, NY: John Wiley & Sons.

15. Padma, S. (2010). "Leadership Attribute Among Women Employees." *Advances in Management*, 3(7), 36–40.

16. Maxwell, J. C. (2010). *Everyone Communicates Few Connect: What the Most Effective People Do Differently*. Nashville, TN: Thomas Nelson, p. 153.

17. Rainey, H. G. (2003). *Understanding and Managing Public Organizations* (3rd ed.). San Francisco, CA: Jossey-Bass, p. 219.

18. Buddhapriya, S. (2009). "Work-Family Challenges and Their Impact on Career Decisions: A Study on Indian Women Professionals." *Vikalpa: The Journal of Decision Makers*, 34(1), 34.

19. Ibid, p. 34.

20. Sauser, 2013, p. 17.

21. Ibid, p. 15.

22. Rainey, 2003, p. 219.

23. Kouzes and Posner, 2010, p. 210.

10: Supporting the Community Through Cultural Awareness

1. Lingenfelter and Mayers, 2003; Livermore, 2009.

2. Livermore, 2009.

3. Lingenfelter and Mayers, 2003.

4. Livermore, 2009, p. 14.

5. Lingenfelter and Mayers, 2003, p. 13.

6. Hall, 1969.

7. Lingenfelter and Mayers, 2003, p. 16

8. Livermore, 2009, p. 99.
9. Ibid, p. 100.
10. Ibid, p. 100.
11. Ibid, p. 63.
12. Chin, C.O., and Gaynier, L. P. (2006). *Global Leadership Competence: A Cultural Intelligence Perspective*. Retrieved from http://www.csuohio.edu/sciences/dept/psychology/ graduate/diversity/htm.
13. Livermore, 2009, p. 69.
14. Thomas, D. (2006). "Domain and Development of Cultural Intelligence: The Importance of Mindfulness." *Group & Organization Management*, 31(1), 92.
15. Friedman, T. (2005). *The World is Flat*. New York, NY: Farrar, Straus and Giroux.
16. Livermore, 2009, pp. 13–14.
17. Ibid, p. 85.
18. Ibid, p. 14.
19. Ibid, pp. 147–148.
20. Weeks, W., Pedersen, P., and Brislin, R. (1977). *A Manual For Structured Experiences For Cross-Cultural Learning*. Yarmouth, ME: Intercultural Press.

21. Livermore, 2009, pp. 212–214.
22. Earley, P. C., Ang, S., and Tan, J. (2006). *CQ: Developing Cultural Intelligence at Work*. Stanford, CA: Stanford Business Books.
23. Livermore, 2009, p. 213.
24. Ibid, p. 239.
25. Storti, C. (1990). *The Art of Crossing Cultures*. Yarmouth, ME: Intercultural Press.
26. Collins, 2009, p. 318.
27. Ibid, p. 320.
28. Livermore, 2009, p. 241.

11: Showing Genuine Concern to the Community

1. Federal Bureau of Investigation. (2002, February 6). *Testimony*. Retrieved from http://www.fbi.gov/news/testimony/the-terrorist-threat-confronting-the-united-states
2. Ibid.
3. Anderson, M. C., Frankovelgia, C., and Hernez-Broome, G. (2009). "Business Leaders Reflect on Coaching Cultures." *In-focus Coaching*, 28(6), 20–23.

4. Caruso, D. R., and Salovey, P. (2012). "Coaching For Emotional Intelligence: MSCEIT." In J. Passmore (Ed.), *Psychometrics in coaching: Using psychological and psychometric tools for development* (2nd ed., pp. 205–223). Philadelphia, PA: Kogan Page.

5. Ibid, p. 207.

6. Andrew, D. (2014). "Genuine Attention and Concern Can Make the Difference in Business." *The Enterprise–Utah's Business Journal, 14*.

7. Gladkova, A. (2010). *Sympathy, Compassion, and Empathy in English and Russian: A Linguistic and Cultural Analysis*. Retrieved from http://0-cap.sagepub.com.library.regent.edu/ content/16/2/267.full.pdf+html

8. Arthur, A. (2014). "Mission, Culture and a Spirituality of the Heart." *Compass*, 48(1), 21–29.

9. Ibid, p. 22.

10. Rost, H. T. D. (1986). *The Golden Rule: A Universal Ethic*. Oxford, UK: Georgia Ronald.

11. Buckley, C. E. (2006). "Golden Rule Reference: Face-to-Face and Virtual." *Reference Librarian*, 45(93), 129–136.

12. Houck, A. (2007). "Hospitality and Courage." *Teaching Theology & Religion*, 10(3), 180.

13. Hotz, K. G. (2007). "They Looked Like Sheep Without a Shepherd: Hospitality and Adult Learners." *Teaching Theology & Religion*, 10(3), 180.

14. McElroy, L. J. (2015). "True Christian Concern." *The Pillar*, 11(1), 1. Retrieved from http://rcg.org/pillar/1101pp-tcc.html

15. Arthur, 2014, p. 25.

16. Ibid, p. 21.

17. Ibid, p. 25.

18. Ibid, p. 22.

19. Sun, S. (2008). "Organizational Culture and Its Themes." *International Journal of Business and Management*, 3(12), 137–141.

20. Morris, E. S. (2009). *Cultural Dimensions and Online Learning Preferences of Asian Students at Oklahoma State University in the United States*. Stillwater: Oklahoma State University.

21. Würtz, E. (2005). "A Cross-Cultural Analysis of Websites From High-Context Cultures and Low-Context Cultures." *Journal of Computer-Mediated Communication*, 11(1), Article 13.

22. Morris, 2009.

23. Changing Minds.org. (2009). *Hall's Cultural Factors*. Retrieved from http://changingminds.org/explanations/culture/hall_culture.htm

24. Morris, 2009.
25. Hall, 1969.
26. Ibid.
27. Ibid.
28. M. C. Anderson et al., 2014, p. 20.
29. Ibid, p. 20.
30. Arthur, 2014, p. 22.
31. Andrew, 2014, p. 14.

12: Encouraging Change

1. Van de Ven, A. H., and Sun, K. (2011). "Breakdowns In Implementing Models of Organization Change." *Academy of Management Perspectives*, 25(3), 58–74.
2. Ibid, p. 59.
3. Ibid, p. 59.
4. Klonek, F. E., Lehmann-Willenbrock, N., and Kauffield, S. (2014). "Dynamics of Resistance to Change: A Sequential Analysis of Change Agents in Action." *Journal of Change Management*, 14(3), 334–360.
5. Collins, 2009, p. 54.
6. Herrington, J., Bonem, M., and Furr, J. H. (2000). *Leading Congregational Change: A Practical Guide*

for the Transformational Journey. San Francisco, CA: Jossey-Bass, p. ix.

7. McEntire, D. A. (2009). "Revolutionary and Evolutionary Change in Emergency Management." *Journal of Business Continuity & Emergency Planning*, 4(1), 69–85.

8. Ibid, p. 77.

9. Herrington et al., 2000.

10. Ibid.

11. Sanders, 1998, pp. 52–53.

12. Ibid, p. 52.

13. Dubrin, A. J. (2004). *Leadership Research Findings, Practice and Skills.* New York, NY: Houghton Mifflin Co., p. 401.

14. Shnall, T. (2013). "The Four Pillars of Encouraging leadership." *Lead Change Group.* Retrieved from http://leadchangegroup.com/the-four-pillars-of-encouraging-leadership/

13: Servant-Leadership Coaching

1. Patterson, K., and Stone, A. G. (2003). "The Seven Habits of Servant Leaders." *The Regent Business Review*, 4, 1–18.